The Homeschool Journey

Susan and Michael Card

HARVEST HOUSE PUBLISHERS
Eugene, Oregon 97402

Cover by Left Coast Design, Portland, Oregon

Cover Photo by Steve Lowry, Nashville, Tennessee

Illustrations by Jan Geloha, Springfield, Oregon

1. *Joy in the Journey* © 1987 Birdwing Music/Mole End Music (ASCAP) Adm. By EMI Christian Music Publishing. All Rights Reserved. Used by Permission.
2. *Poem of Your Life* © 1994 Birdwing Music (ASCAP) Adm. By EMI Christian Music Publishing. All Rights Reserved. Used by Permission.
3. *Chorus of Faith* © 1994 Birdwing Music/Davaub Music (ASCAP) Adm. By EMI Christian Music Publishing. All Rights Reserved. Used by Permission.
4. *Nathan's Song* © 1993 Birdwing Music (ASCAP) Adm. By EMI Christian Music Publishing. All Rights Reserved. Used by Permission.
5. *Will You Not Listen* © 1992 Birdwing Music (ASCAP) Adm. By EMI Christian Music Publishing. All Rights Reserved. Used by Permission.
6. *So Many Books* © 1992 Birdwing Music (ASCAP) Adm. By EMI Christian Music Publishing. All Rights Reserved. Used by Permission.
7. *Sunrise of Your Smile* © 1994 Birdwing Music/Davaub Music (ASCAP) Adm. By EMI Christian Music Publishing. All Rights Reserved. Used by Permission.
8. *Know You In The Now* © 1988 Birdwing Music/Mole End Music (ASCAP) Adm. By EMI Christian Music Publishing. All Rights Reserved. Used by Permission.
9. *That's What Faith Must Be* © 1988 Birdwing Music/Mole End Music (ASCAP) Adm. By EMI Christian Music Publishing. All Rights Reserved. Used by Permission.

THE HOMESCHOOL JOURNEY
Copyright © 1997 by Susan Card
Published by Harvest House Publishers
Eugene, Oregon 97402

Library of Congress Cataloging-in-Publication Data

Card, Susan, 1960-
    The homeschool journey / Susan Card with Michael Card.
        p.   cm.
    Includes bibliographical references.
    ISBN 1-56507-568-4
    1. Home schooling—United States—Case studies. 2. Christian education—United States—Case studies. 3. Card, Susan, 1960- . 4. Card, Michael, 1957- . I. Card, Michael, 1957- . II. Title.
LC40.C37 1997   97-7435
371.04'2'0973—dc21   CIP

This book is lovingly dedicated to our parents:
J. H. and Nancy Kepley
and
Bill and Ailene Card

Acknowledgments

Many thanks to:

Elizabeth Maranise for so many years of your unspoken kindness and for bringing order into disorder.

Kelli Wagener for adapting so well and so willingly. You have been a blessing to our home.

Our homeschool community and friends: Terry and Susan Comer, Jim and Dawn Taylor, Andy and Valerie McDaniel, Melvin and Edie Spain.

Harvest House Publishers for being the most gracious publishing staff, especially Terry Glaspey and Carolyn McCready.

Michael Card Music staff for all the extras, but most of all for your love and support: Jonathon Duda, Kim Dye, Barbara Emerson, Malcom Greenwood, Pat Moody (thanks for trading places), Rinda Smith, and Mitch White.

My special support group who helped bear the burden: Ken Cope (the best "listener" I know), Jeff and Kristi Kepley, Fran King, Scott Roley, Pastor Scotty and Darlene Smith, Debby Stewart, and Stevie Waltrip.

Bill and Brenda Lane, your love and wisdom are still very present.

Brennan Manning for the special phone call that came at just the right time.

Most of all to Katherine, Will, Nathan, and Maggie for being mine to love and care for. And most especially to Michael (my best friend as well as husband), who bore most of the burden—my absence. Thank you for running interference, for editing, for the best cups of coffee, for staying up late with me, for putting your project down to take care of so many details on our behalf. I am more than glad to trade places! I love you!

Contents

1. Our Journey Begins   9

2. Our Foundation. 23

3. A Vision for Character 45

4. A Walk with Creativity. 59

5. Stepping in Time to the Music. 91

6. A Steep Path to Climb 109

7. Companions on the Journey 131

8. Feeding the Mind 147

9. Some Questions About Homeschooling 169

   Recommended Resources. 185

   Scripture Passages Illustrated
   by Michael Card Songs. 209

   Epilogue. 213

Preface

*A*braham Heschel warns against becoming a "stranger to your child's soul." For Susan and me those few words contain the essence of why we homeschool. There are a thousand peripheral reasons: to enhance the quality of education which may be lacking in the public or private schools, to engrain spiritual and moral values, and so on. The list is endless, but at the heart of it all there is the concern for the souls of our children, that they might be shaped, sheltered, and encouraged. And that we, as parents, may not become estranged from them in the process.

Love is at the heart of caring for a soul, and the best way to show someone you love him is to listen to him. Susan consistently amazes me by her ability to listen to the subtleties of the lives of our four children. By using this gift she determines which approach will be best to "break through" to each individual child. And therein lies the best reason for her to have written this book. As we walked together during the writing of it, she constantly struggled with misgivings about her own abilities as a writer, with all the voices in her head telling her she couldn't do it and why. But the gift this book has to offer is not essentially a literary one. It contains the journaling of a godly woman who has lovingly sought to open the door of the life of each of her children. It describes the struggles involved in the process, as well as the benefits. For those of you who are already on the journey called homeschooling, hopefully there will be insights with which your hearts will resonate. For those of you who are standing at the beginning of the road, this book will serve as a voice of one who has gone ahead and calls back to tell you which steps to take and which to avoid.

Another value of Susan's work here is her ability to see which issues we need to be dogmatically passionate about and which ones are a matter of mere personal choice. It seems to me that many homeschooling books fail in this. They become dogmatic about points which are secondary in nature to the heart of homeschooling. In doing this, they drive many prospective homeschool parents away from the adventure. For the foundation of the homeschooling movement is the freedom of the parents to make those choices which best suit their children. When we are robbed of this freedom, we are robbed of much of the joy of homeschooling.

Finally, let me say that during the months while she was working on this manuscript, Katie, Will, Nate, Maggie, and I were made aware by her absence of just how much we need Susan, of how mundane our lives can become without the gentle touch of her presence in the house. But it was a sacrifice we are glad to have made if this book will strengthen your resolve to either push on with your homeschooling or make your first steps in that direction.

—Michael Card

ONE

Our Journey Begins

There is a joy in the journey
There's a light we can love on the way
There is a wonder and wildness to life
and freedom for those who obey

Lyric from "Joy in the Journey"/*Joy in the Journey*
Words and Music by Michael Card
Used by permission

*O*ne cold winter day early in our marriage, Michael and I were at his parents' home celebrating Thanksgiving. When we had finished with the meal and everyone else was sitting around talking or trying to recover from the immense feast we had just enjoyed, I moved into the room off the kitchen to play with our nephew, Daniel. I thought that it might be fun to sit with him and work a puzzle. The only one available was a large wooden map of the United States, which had all the states labeled with their names. We dumped the pieces on the floor and I said, "Why don't you show me where the pieces go? If you get stuck, I'll help you." Putting the border together was simple enough, but as we tried to fill in the middle pieces, we ran into problems.

"Where does this go?" he would ask, expecting an authoritative adult answer, but I found that my geography was not as good as I had thought. More than once "dear auntie" found that she was not quite sure where the pieces belonged. Where should Colorado be placed in relation to Nebraska? Daniel finally got tired of waiting for me to figure it out and left to play with his train.

As I sat there staring at the unfinished puzzle, I found myself thinking back to a college course called Pathophysiology that I had taken the year before, and to one day in particular when our test scores were to be returned. The room was full of nursing students, all working toward their bachelor's degree. With his arms folded, our professor sat on a stool in front of us. He had greeted no one as we entered class that day, keeping a deliberate silence which informed us that we had not done very well. We sat timidly in our chairs awaiting the results.

The poor outcome came as no surprise to us. On our last exam, instead of giving the normal exam format, he had surprised us by asking only one question. Our entire six weeks of study would ride on giving a detailed description of an immunological process of which I cannot now even remember the name. When the test had been handed out, a petrified stillness had settled over the room. Was he kidding? Put this in our own words?

"I am disgusted," he said. "I sit in front of an entire class of students who cannot write in their own words what we have discussed in detail for weeks! We have failed as educators if you cannot give the information back. These results prove to me that you have no understanding of what I have been teaching. According to what I see on these exams, the last few weeks have been a waste of my time." Although my heart and my pride were wounded, I could not argue with the truth of his words. For the first time, a light came on. His chastising drove home the essence of what education is supposed to be.

To be educated is not merely to have the ability to answer multiple-choice questions on a test. True education is a process of digestion, where knowledge becomes your own as you take information in, ponder it, grapple with it, and separate the truth from the falsehoods. If you really have knowledge, you should be able to translate it to other people. Once you can explain what you know, you are much closer to true understanding. Simple memorization is not enough. The purpose of education is not to harbor facts with our minds, but to comprehend truths. All the memorized facts come to life only as we truly understand them. And we understand them only when we become disciplined enough to ponder, to consider, to ask questions.

Although I still did not understand the immunological system as I should, I gained that day a deeper understanding of the purpose of learning. My professor was right to be disgusted, but the members of that class full of nurses were the living results of the educational systems we had passed through. We were mostly registered nurses who had already passed our state boards, but our education was deficient in that we were able to memorize material without it really entering our understanding.

My degree and professional title were very much on my mind as I sat with Colorado in my hand, trying to place it properly in my nephew's puzzle. How was it that I knew so little about something as fundamental as geography? I was a nurse, a well-educated person, but I had slipped through the educational system without learning how to learn. As I thought about my own children, I wanted something better for them.

My own parents had encouraged good education and thought it was accomplished when report cards revealed A's and B's. What I had come to realize is that education is more than schooling—it is a way of life.

And where better to learn that way of life than in the home? Home is a place of comfort and healing, a place of safety and security. And from this secure outpost we can explore our world. Home is where great things are spoken and where our imaginations are unleashed to explore and wander in the presence of warm, loving companions who both encourage us and teach us what areas are best left unexplored. Home is where you learn discipline and are disciplined, because home is where you are loved.

Choices in Education

Seven years into our marriage, Michael and I found ourselves faced with deciding how we would educate our children. Knowing that early registration was necessary in most cases, I began exploring the possible choices—both public and private—when our daughter Katie was only four years old.

The option of homeschooling was brought to my attention by three of my friends who had children who were older than mine. They were all teaching their children at home. As I had the privilege of spending time with them, I was exposed to a new way of schooling that encouraged me in my belief that the home was the best place for learning to take place. They gave me a direction as well as a vision for implementing what seemed natural and right to me: extending the responsibility I felt for nurturing and training my children to the realm of their education.

What I found interesting in observing these three homeschooling families was that they all had the same goal, though their motivations and methods were very different. The goal was to provide a great education for their children by supplying a warm and loving environment in which to learn—an environment that included close and active parental participation. They wanted to create an atmosphere free from the negative influences of our culture, to eliminate certain distractions to moral and intellectual growth, and to protect their children from temptations they were not yet prepared to face. This was a vision that I longed to make a reality in my own home, with my own children.

Friends and Mentors

I remember the dry-erase board hanging in Frances's kitchen, and the children sitting quietly at the table engrossed in their schoolwork as I looked out the window at her beautiful roses. Frances always had the windows open at this time of year, and the peacefulness and serenity of the setting just seemed so right, as fresh as the breezes blowing through her kitchen window. This seemed like the most natural environment in which to educate a child. The sounds wafting in from outdoors enhanced the moment, and I was consumed with the desire to re-create this moment, this atmosphere, this way of life in my own home.

Frances's decision to teach her children at home had been a recent one, and we had not yet had the opportunity to talk it over. But it seemed so right. It seemed like the logical decision someone with her convictions would make. We had been long-time friends after meeting in a Bible study years before I had any children. We had shared a love for horses, for art, and for books. In her home, the television had been removed from its place of prominence. Instead of it being the center of her living room, she and her husband kept the television put away, only letting the children see videos on the weekends. The focus of her living room was a book-lined wall.

Their home was focused on and motivated by great literature. Frances was an avid reader herself and took much delight in reading to her children. Throughout the week the children were read to and encouraged to read. Reading was an activity as naturally integrated into the average day as eating a meal. Losing oneself in the pages of a book was a common pastime for the whole family. Our exposure to this family encouraged us to pursue endeavors such as this. Their example served as a warm invitation to live a lifestyle of teaching our children at home.

Frances was not my only positive influence in the direction of homeschooling. There was also Ingrid. Ingrid, when in her element, was a picture of sheer joy. She was the most creative person I knew, and her home and children were a reflection of this. She saw the artistry in everyday activities, applying her creativity to the details of every aspect of her life. A simple meal or a flower garden could reflect her love of beauty and her creative spirit. When she taught in her home, her girls became participants, examples, and helpers. Ingrid was a ballet teacher, and her life was reflective of a dance. Her children were the rich benefactors of her life's freedom, movement, and creativity. I cherished this for my own children.

Linda was a woman of purpose. Her focus and motivation were biblical. Her primary goal was to provide an atmosphere that protected her children from temptations and influences they were not yet prepared to face. She wanted to preserve their innocence and at the same time educate them with a solid biblical foundation. Her goal was to keep them at home until the sixth grade and then, once sure of who they were in the context of their parents and the Christian community, she and her husband would send them to a public or private school to finish their education.

Though each of these women followed a different path, they shared the goal of providing the best experience for their children. Watching how each of these homes operated gave me the confidence to find my own way. They primed the pump of my imagination.

Other mentors were found in books. For Christmas one year, Frances gave me a copy of *Homegrown Kids* by Raymond and Dorothy Moore. I found this book to be very encouraging. The Moores gave validation to the natural and simple things of home life and helped me to appreciate more deeply the way my parents had raised me. They helped me to realize how much our culture had lost in its striving for prestige and power. I had come to believe that my value to society was tied up in my degrees, my position, my accomplishments. I had to be something to be somebody. But though the Moores do encourage the pursuit of excellence, it is always in the context of the warmth of family life. Also, their thorough research into the effectiveness of home-based education satisfied the need I had to feel that I was on solid ground, that I was not putting my children at risk in making my decision to homeschool.

Mary Pride's *The Way Back Home* was another helpful book. When I saw her at a seminar I attended, she spoke of the awful state of public education. The schools were facing numbers of dilemmas for which solutions were still being sought. I became convinced that I could not put my children into the public school system and be confident that they were in the best situation. It became clear to me that Michael and I would have to roll up our sleeves along with many other parents and make a contribution to the community rather than simply adding more children to the culturally decaying pot.

But the book that had the greatest influence on me was Susan Schaeffer Macaulay's *For the Children's Sake*. It was as if Susan herself had set me aside and said, "Now, I want you to be a big girl and start thinking for yourself. Reflect on your past. Are you satisfied with your own education? Watch your children and observe. Are they free in their play, or are they tired, bored, and unimaginative?" By introducing the modern homeschooling movement to the thoughts of nineteenth-century English educator Charlotte Mason, Susan has provided us with a wonderful and freeing approach to teaching. Susan convinced me that my natural instincts were right and that I could do it. The highest goals I had for my children could be reached by teaching them at home.

The Importance of a Mentor

If you are serious about homeschooling, I would encourage you to find someone with experience to help you on your way. I cannot stress enough the importance of having someone to function as a mentor. You do not need someone who will force their opinions and preferences upon you, but rather, someone who will listen to what your unique needs are and help you tap into the resources necessary for improving your own teaching experience.

Such a person in my life is Valerie McDaniel. When I first came to know her, she was my daughter's Sunday school teacher. In a certain sense, she has become my teacher as well. In her mind, homeschooling began the day her children were born. It is a way of life for her, and she was gracious enough to open up for me a window into that lifestyle. Valerie took me under her wing and walked me through curriculum choices and other important decisions, introduced me to helpful seminars, and offered a listening ear whenever perplexing questions arose. Because she had an unshakable conviction that this was the best way to educate her children, she was a rock of strength during my times of insecurity. And I was not the only one to whom she sacrificially gave her time and energy. Many women have been encouraged to begin homeschooling or have been supported during times of frustration by her gift of mentoring.

What made Valerie such a great mentor is that she did not try to force me into her way of doing things. In fact, I seldom did things exactly as she had done them. She knew the truth that the parent is the one who is most in tune with what his or her children need. As a parent you can and should find what works best for you.

I have not written this book to tell you how it should be done. Instead, like my mentors did for me, I want to give you a window into my own homeschooling experiences. I want to help you see what has worked for my children and challenge you to gain a deeper and richer vision for your own. We have the awesome responsibility as parents to cooperate with God in building strong character in our children and helping them to be the kind of people both we and God want them to be.

Michael's Perspective

What inevitably lies at the root of many families' decision to homeschool is their own experiences of school in growing up. My own experiences were, for the most part, positive. I was not driven away from learning by public school, but instead was drawn toward learning by my experience at home. Though I attended public school, in reality I received much of my own education at home.

My earliest memories of home are all associated not with events but with the songs and stories that surrounded me as a child: my father's jazz band practicing in the basement; the cigarette smoke drifting up the stairs along with the melodies (and, to my disappointment, no words!); my mother's sad lullabies: "My child it's growing dark, I'd rather you'd come in . . ."; the folk records playing on my brother's mono record player (these were the days before stereo!). I was captured by the words, sung or unsung. Listening to the lyrics of "Puff the Magic Dragon," I would find myself weeping without knowing why, except that in-between the words I sensed the loss of something universal, something that I, too, would lose someday.

Whether they are homeschooled or not, our children need us to listen to their lives. My mother listened to me and my life, and bought me my first guitar. On long trips she would ask my sister and me to sing our songs to her. By God's grace, from my earliest days those around me seemed to understand my love affair with words. They listened to mine and spoke wonderful words of encouragement to me.

The love for words was also fostered by the other great legacy of my home: books. Both of my grandfathers had been bookish men, and so remnants of their libraries lined the cherry shelves of our home. My father read widely in archaeology, astronomy, history, and physics, as well as the endless journals and medical books of his profession.

Both my parents were steeped in the classics. They remembered book plots and characters so vividly that they became real to me. A change would come over the voices of my father and mother whenever either of them would begin to talk about this or that novel or poem. "Ailene Kilmer!" my mother would whisper with reverence, or "Dumas!" or "Tolstoy!" or "Melville!" Their tone would modulate and echo something manifestly interesting.

Britannica, *American History*, and *Science Yearbooks* were school to me every bit as much as the public institutions where I spent my days. I remember leafing through the pages of the illustrated encyclopedias, and to this day I recognize concepts from these simple line drawings.

All this was merely the countdown for me, the laying of foundations, the building of a rocket ship that would carry me elsewhere. The fuse was lit by a high school English teacher, Mrs. Zuccarello, a lovely Southern lady of the old school—warm, gentle, and capable of handling even the sarcastic students who would badger her in class as she tried to do her miraculous work. The match she laid to the fuse of my imagination was *The Count of Monte Cristo* by Alexandre Dumas. The timing was perfect for me. (The impact of good books is often as much a matter of timing as anything else.) My world would never be the same.

With that novel, my real education began. The dictionaries and encyclopedias had made ready the vocabulary. The picture books and the atlases had provided the settings. The music played in our home had taught me to hear the hidden music of the novel. Nothing would ever seem ordinary again.

But the question of timing is so important. *The Count of Monte Cristo* had been sitting on our shelves at home for as long as I could remember. I can see to this day the lettering on the leather spine as it leaned against another of the classics on the shelf. My mother had spoken in her special tone of voice about Edmund Dante and his struggle with revenge. But it had not been the right time for me. There are seasons in a child's growth that the parent must come to understand. There is the spring of lullabies and letters and the summer of simple songs, but in time the year will progress into the harvest season where the door of imagination will swing wide open to the classics of literature and great music.

Why do I tell you of these memories? Because I think they reveal a great deal about our decision to homeschool.

In my home, I learned the importance of creating an atmosphere of a home filled with resources where exploring was always encouraged. None of the shelves of the library were off-limits to us. As far back as I can remember, those shelves were like fields filled with hidden treasures.

Also, I learned that whatever it is that God has created us to be will usually begin to surface early in a child's life. This means we must listen very carefully to the lives of our children and to what God is telling us about them. My own parents were attentive to my own growing love affair with words and sensitive to how God might use my developing gifts. Homeschool families have a special advantage in this area because every aspect of training and nurturing the child is under the parents' direct attention.

Of course, in all this discussion of the classics and words we cannot forget the Word of God. Norman Maclean, in his short story "A River Runs Through It," speaks of what lies beneath the ancient rocks of the river, and that is the Word of God. For me, the novels were the river, beneath which the Word of God provided the channeling force.

It was there all along in the "Christ figures" who struggled, and sacrificed, and served. It was there in the beauty of the words themselves—a reflection of the beauty of the Word. When the call to the Word finally came, I was ready to hear, to imagine, and to ask the right questions of it. In *Lost Horizon*, I had journeyed to meet the ancient wisdom of God, shrouded in incense and mystery. I had experienced the zeal that God would require of me in the story of Ahab and the white whale. In Edmund Dante's final reconciliation with God, I had already tasted my own. In the stories of the folk songs I had grown up with, I learned to listen to the music beneath the words. And all these hearings and experiences, sounds and tastes and smells, serve me to this day.

And so I look to my own home and my own children, and pray that God will give me the grace to learn to listen to their lives. I ask for patience to wait for the opportune time to open this or that door. And both Susan and I long to create a home with the kind of atmosphere, the kind of peace, the kind of loving-kindness where all this might happen for our children, just as it did for us.

Two

Our Foundation

Sing it with your life, sing with your heart
Make melody with the words of your mouth
But mind that you listen, tell it to others
Hear the chorus of faith
Live the chorus of faith

Lyric from "Chorus of Faith"/*Joy in the Journey*
Words by Michael Card/Music by Phil Naish
Used by permission

*U*ltimately, the decision to teach our children at home is a response to our faith in Christ. In our journey of faith, the Lord has entrusted Michael and me with four children for whom we are responsible. Proverbs 22:6 is clear about what that responsibility is: "Train a child in the way he should go, and when he is old he will not turn from it." Every parent should respond to this call of responsibility out of obedience to the Lord. How the training takes place is up to the parents. There are many different and still very effective ways to achieve the same end. For our family, the training process is primarily taken care of at home, with some outside supplements. For other families, education is primarily taken care of in a school, with the parents supplementing. Whichever direction you decide to go, enter it prayerfully, keeping a watchful eye on your child's development.

Training our children means that we must be aware of those elements in our culture which cause stumbling blocks to our child's spiritual development. So many of our modern conveniences can become the source of a multitude of distractions. As a society, even among Christians, our gaze is not fixed on the Lord as much as it is on the television screen. Too often, instead of working through our problems, we merely distract ourselves with a round of

video games. We seem to have lost the ability to balance our modern pleasures with an earnest pursuit of the Almighty, and are ill-equipped to face the many challenges of life. By the way that we deal with these areas, we set an example for our children. Our priorities are evident in our actions.

Faith in Jesus Christ is the foundation of our home. Michael has taken the lead in trying to make certain that our home is thoroughly "Christ-centered," rather than just being "religious." In our home, we attempt to make Christ the center of everything in our lives, whether it be living out His example of servanthood, seeing His handiwork in creation, or living out His presence as we read Scripture together. Every issue that comes up and every question that arises is put to this test: Am I living in conformity to the character and will of Christ? In other words, it is not just an intellectual or emotional commitment to the Lord. It is the willingness to transform our lifestyle so that it is pleasing to Him. Our hope is to reflect His life through our own. Many people feel that homeschooling is a radical choice for a family to make, but I do not think so. I think that it is a perfectly natural choice for a family that wants to be Christ-centered. Our commitment to homeschooling stretches us to go beyond our culture's godless and morally bankrupt value system. But we do not live a radical lifestyle because we homeschool; we homeschool because of the radical nature of our faith. It stretches us to be different, to go beyond "the normal." and live in obedience to God and His Word. For us, though homeschooling may be "different," it is part of our radical obedience.

Faith for the Journey

How can we best prepare ourselves and our children for succeeding in life? Hebrews 11 teaches us clearly that faith should be the center of our lives. *Faith* is a word that many people use to mean many different things, but Hebrews 11:1 gives us the best definition: "being sure of what we hope for and certain of what we do not see." Michael has written of this in one of his songs:

> *To hear with my heart*
> *To see with my soul*
> *To be guided by a hand*
> *I cannot hold*
> *To trust in a way that I*
> *cannot see*
> *That's what faith must be**

But how does such a faith influence the way we raise and educate our children? I think that there are several ways in which faith provides for us.

First, faith helps us understand that God created the universe, and that He made it out of nothing. Maggie, our youngest, is just three. This very night we read a bedtime story that asked, "Who made the cow? Who made the pig? The duck? The sheep? The chickens?" Maggie knew the answer without my having to read it, because we teach our children, from the earliest possible age, the origin of all that is around them. The snow that fell this Christmas past, the birds that flock to the feeders, the clouds looming overhead—all of these have a Creator. Our faith in a beginning initiated by God gives us the response to our children's question of "Who made this?" The answer is, "God did."

---

* Lyric from "That's What Faith Must Be"/*Present Reality*/Words and Music by
  Michael Card

Second, faith gives us the ability to live sacrificially. Every parent who has chosen this path knows that home-schooling is a choice that necessitates sacrifice! For me, the largest sacrifice may be in the area of solitude. I am a person who really craves times alone. But for those who choose to teach at home, there are all-too-few times of true solitude and quiet. Other parents may have different areas where they must sacrifice their own preferences and time. But faith enables us to put ourselves aside for this all to brief season of our lives.

Third, faith gives us the ability to obey. Hebrews 11:8 says, "By faith Abraham, when called to go to a place he would later receive as his inheritance, obeyed and went, even though he did not know where he was going." Imagine how difficult that must have been! Obedience is rarely easy. I find that making my children obey is very difficult. How much easier it would be to just let some of their bad behavior slip by me as though I did not notice, rather than facing

their resistance to change in the process of teaching them right from wrong. It requires discipline to discipline! It can be a tiring process, but I do it out of obedience to the Lord. Without faith, I would not have the fear of displeasing a holy God to motivate me.

Fourth, faith gives us a longing for heaven. It is our desire to give our children a sense of their future with the Lord. When they were still quite young, Will and Katie were having breakfast one morning when Will suddenly asked, "Mom, are there toys in heaven?" Before I could answer, Katie jumped in. "Will," she scolded, "God doesn't allow toys in heaven, because He doesn't want us to love our toys more than Him." The very suggestion made her indignant. Will pondered her answer for a moment, while I tried to suppress a smile. "Well," he said, thinking of his favorite stuffed animal, "when I die, I'm going to grab my brontosaurus!" It was evident to me from both responses that we had succeeded in planting the reality of heaven within our children's hearts. But to even imagine heaven at all is a gift of faith. Michael and I receive many letters from parents who have lost their children, but find comfort in knowing that they are with the Lord. Faith gives us the confidence, in the midst of our struggles, that Jesus has gone to prepare a place for us.

Fifth, faith gives us courage. It is so easy to become captive to the gripping paralysis of fear. As a homeschooling parent, I can sometimes begin to be fearful about what I am doing. But then I remember those who have gone before me, the pioneers of the homeschooling movement, who refused to give way to government restrictions and fought for the right to teach their own children. I am part of a generation of parents who are the benefactors of people who embraced their convictions, stood their ground, and resisted fear, sometimes to the point of being imprisoned for their beliefs. This same kind of courage is needed on a daily basis as we face our insecurities and shortcomings as parents and teachers. Courage is necessary when the voices of skepticism try to convince us that we, as parents, cannot do the job and that we must leave it to the "professionals."

Sixth, faith gives us the ability to withstand persecution. For believers in some parts of our world, being persecuted for their faith is a part of everyday life. It will most likely be a reality for all of us someday. It is only through faith that we can have the strength to endure the struggles that may lie ahead. And when your child is in a difficult situation, he needs a living faith to know where to turn.

Finally, and most important, faith pleases God. Without it, we would never be able to come to Him as true believers or seek Him earnestly. It is very important, even when your children are quite young, to encourage them to express their faith. Let them know that God is very pleased when they take Him at His word.

If you are already homeschooling, or even if you are just considering it, you will need the gift of faith to succeed. Before you set your heart and mind to the task, embrace the faith that comes from a relationship with God. It will give you the motivation to persevere, strength in times of hardship, and a clear path for your children to follow as they begin their personal journey. It is by faith that we forge ahead in the huge task of raising our children!

Knowing the Shepherd's Voice

Jesus once told a parable to illustrate how important it was for His followers to listen for His voice:

> I tell you the truth, the man who does not enter the sheep pen by the gate, but climbs in by some other way, is a thief and a robber. The man who enters by the gate is the shepherd of his sheep. The watchman opens the gate for him, and the sheep listen to his voice. He calls his own sheep by name and leads them out. When he has brought out all his own, he goes on ahead of them, and his sheep follow him because they know his voice. But they will never follow a stranger; in fact, they will run away from him because they do not recognize a stranger's voice (John 10:1-5).

This is why studying the Bible is such an important part of our homeschooling. Our ultimate goal in teaching the Bible is to introduce our children to the Good Shepherd and help them to recognize His voice. It is so easy for us to get distracted by other voices! Billy Graham in his book *Angels: God's Secret Agents* notes that many people—even Christians—are so preoccupied with the enemy that they become distracted from attending to the Lord. While still quite young, I was encouraged to stay focused on the Lord and become as familiar with Him as I could. I have followed this advice in raising my own children.

One of the great advantages in homeschooling is having the opportunity to teach the Bible with as much emphasis as you would give to any other subject. On a daily basis we integrate Bible lessons and character building into our educational experience. From the lessons of Scripture, our children are confronted by important questions such as:

How are we treating each other within the family?
Are we learning to control our anger?
Are we sharing with one another?
What is our attitude when we are asked to do some thing we really don't want to do?
How does Jesus expect us to behave?

Ultimately, the goal is that we learn to hear the echo of His voice resonating in our hearts and minds as He teaches us to lay down our nets and follow Him.

Making Bible Study Real

The great danger in teaching the Bible as part of your curriculum is that you can fall prey to teaching facts without implementing the truths they point to. Teaching the Bible is not done by pounding away at required lessons and forcing a great deal of Scripture memorization. But if you are aware and if you listen to your own life, there are lessons every day that point to spiritual implications. If we maintain that delicate awareness, life experience and the Scriptures speak together in beautiful harmony. To teach our faith we must intricately weave the two together with creativity and joy.

Sometimes a story from the Bible can help our children connect their experiences with scriptural teaching. We reached a point in our schooling last year where Katie and Will were always grumbling about doing their schoolwork. "Why do we have to?" was always on the tips of their tongues, no matter what the task assigned to them. Whether it be a school assignment, cleaning their rooms, or just asking them to be nice to one another, it was a constant refrain day after day. They were disrespectful and, because Michael was touring at this time, I was left to deal with it by myself. I sorely missed his authority.

We were working on a handwriting exercise one morning, and they were casting their furrowed brows my way, with an attitude that combined frustration with complaining. I was really getting tired of this resistance, but instead of shutting them down emotionally by my own burst of frustration, as I had the day before, I decided that I would answer their question, "Why?" The Lord was good enough to bring a story to my mind which would reply to their constant nagging.

"Okay," I said, "put your pencils down and come outside with me." They looked up, a little surprised and maybe a touch worried. I decided that the change of scenery would do us all some good, and the fresh air might just freshen all our attitudes!

As we sat on the porch together, we snuggled close and I reassured them that I loved them, even when their attitudes were out of line. I also told them that I expected them to exercise some self-control and told them the story the Lord brought to mind to illustrate the point.

"You know how you two always ask me 'Why?' no matter what I ask you to do, whether it be cleaning your room, studying your math, or simply obeying?"

They nodded grudging assent.

"Well, do you remember the story about Samuel and Eli?" I knew they did, as we had just read that particular story from their Bible storybook a few days earlier.

"Yes," they said, "we remember."

"Tell me about Samuel," I ventured. "Was he obedient to the Lord? What about Eli's two sons? What were they like?" I slowly drew the story from their own lips. After each question, I let them tell me a little more of the story.

"Did Eli make his sons obey? Did he honor the Lord above his sons?"

They answered back quickly, pleased with themselves for how well they remembered. Now I prepared to bring my point home.

"Was God pleased with Eli? How do you know?"

They answered that God was not pleased and that Eli was punished.

With my lesson almost over, I prepared one final question: "Would God be pleased with me if I did not make you obey?"

From the look on their faces, I knew that the point had struck home.

"Of course He wouldn't be pleased. So do you see that my enforcing rules at home is part of my obedience to the Lord? Do you see the trouble we could run into if we chose to do otherwise?"

We prayed together a prayer of apology, watched the Bible videotape on Samuel, and then resumed our studies, having found the answer to the question, "Why?" We must obey because God says so.

Scripture provides us with the voice of the Shepherd. It serves as a living letter speaking to us in its own miraculous way. By reading devotions together and sharing relevant experiences, you model for your children how to interact with Jesus on a personal level. Familiarity with Jesus comes from consistent reading of what He had to say and what was said about Him. As early as is practical for your children, read the Bible to them and then encourage them to read it for themselves. There is no substitution when it comes to growing spiritually. As they grow, we can see its fruit in the lives of our children. Their ability to apply the truth of the gospel to their lives is operating on a surprisingly mature level. Our children have already surpassed the spiritual understanding that Michael and I had when we were their age.

Integrity and Quality

When Michael and I first began reading books aloud to Katie on a regular basis, we found that there was no shortage of great books with colorful and lively illustrations. She would sit entranced at the marvelous stories and the eye-catching artwork. But when it came to choosing Bible storybooks that would capture her attention, we found that many of the available choices were disappointing both to her and to us. Often we came up empty-handed. Most of the Bible storybooks simply failed to capture her imagination. We became frustrated when we realized that she knew more about Winnie the Pooh and was more enamored with him than with any person she had been introduced to in the Bible.

Fortunately, the selection of quality Bible storybooks has greatly improved in the last few years. There are an abundance of these books being published that are written and illustrated with children in mind. Not all of them are of the highest quality, but an increasing number are being produced that wed together accuracy, the ability to interest the child, and a true aesthetic quality. We should always try to offer our children the best that is available.

The problem with many materials for children is that they "talk down" to the kids. Like many other homeschool parents, Michael and I have found that you do not need to talk down to your children in order to effectively teach them. In fact, they seem to respond better when they are given a bit of a challenge. Nor does artwork need to betray good taste in order to be captivating. As parents, we should strive to provide a nurturing environment that will help our children develop both a critical mind for detecting truth and a critical eye for appreciating beauty. At one time Michael struggled with the fact that some of the most widely admired Christian music and writing was of dubious artistic quality, showing very little creativity and originality. His temptation was to be critical. Instead, he remembered the words of one of his college professors, William Lane, who had said to him, "Let the excellence of your work be your protest." These wise words now hang in Michael's recording studio as a reminder to resist the temptation to compromise the integrity of quality workmanship.

There is no activity that so calls for integrity and quality of workmanship as raising children. And when we are seeking to educate them as well, the task only grows more challenging. But for what area of education could these qualities be more important than when we turn to teaching them the great spiritual truths of Scripture?

When we treat our children as intelligent and gifted human beings, they usually respond in that manner. How much better this is than some sort of silly mental or visual gymnastics! We should be honest and direct in our conversation. But when it comes to storytelling, then we can let our hair down and be just as animated as we please.

Katie has, for the most part, outgrown Pooh—though she occasionally still enjoys hearing the stories. Her interest in the people of the Bible, though, continues to grow as a result of trying to mix integrity, artfulness, and entertainment together in our reading of the Bible.

Teaching the Bible

There are many good and effective ways to teach the Bible. We have used many different methods over the years. One of the beauties of homeschooling is that we have the freedom to adapt to meet the needs of the entire family. Hopefully, some of what I have found helpful will also prove helpful to you.

I have found that it is most profitable to approach the Bible with two different mind-sets: the devotional and the historical. Until we have looked at Scripture from both of these angles, we have not done justice to the message that is contained there.

In the devotional approach, I read with mind and heart in a listening mode. I am trying to hear what the familiar voice of the Shepherd is speaking to me. What is it that He would say to me in the present moment? Michael wrote of this in one of his songs, called "Present Reality":

> Echo of history
> A light so many strain to see
> The One we talk so much about
> But rarely ever live it out
>
> Lord I long to see
> Your presence in reality
> But I don't know how
> Let me know you in the now.

But not only do we want our children to learn to read in such a way as to hear the voice of the Shepherd, we also want them to know how God has revealed Himself to His people in the course of history. The historical is the second approach we must take to the Bible. We need to understand the characters of the Bible in the context of the times in which they lived: their race, culture, and geographical settings. This takes a little more time than the purely devotional reading, but it is critical if we and our children are to really understand the message of the Scriptures.

We must work to form a bridge between our own experiences and those which we read of in the Bible. This will actually enhance our personal experiences. When our children know the facts about Jesus, it can lead to knowing Him that much better. For instance, when we read that Jesus entered the home of Zacchaeus, the dishonest tax collector, it should teach us the necessity of being gracious and loving, even to the disobedient. His compassion for the sick and suffering should provide a model for our own growth in caring, and the fact that Jesus was of a different race from us should help us to rid ourselves of our prejudices. Of course, we could go on and on about what we can learn as we look at the historical context and then listen to how that applies to our "present reality."

What Has Worked for Us

Such thoughts as those above are all well and good, but may leave some readers asking the question, "But how do I do it?" I thought that it might be helpful to give you some specifics about what we have done and what has worked for us. Keep in mind that our own children are still in the elementary grades, so this section may not be as helpful to those with older children.

Our day begins with devotions around the breakfast table. I thought that this would be a good place to introduce the people, places, and events of the Bible by reading from a Bible storybook. The one that both I and the children have most appreciated is *My Very First Bible* (published by Harvest House). What makes this book so good is that the illustrations are lively and dramatic, and the stories short, but captivating. We read straight through this book with a great deal of enjoyment. We also read through *The Beginner's Bible* (published by Zondervan). *The Story of the Bible* (published by Eerdmans) is another one we tried, but with not as much success. It's a great storybook, but seems to be a little beyond the reach of my younger children.

For a while, we put the Bible storybooks aside and began to read the Miller series by Mildred A. Martin (published by Green Pastures Press). These wonderful little books about the daily lives of an Amish family serve to put Scripture into the context of daily living, giving powerful examples of how to apply the Bible to our lives in a practical way. Three of her books that we have enjoyed are

Storytime and the Millers, devotional stories for children ages 4-8; *Wisdom and the Millers,* devotional stories from Proverbs for children ages 6-13; and *Prudence and the Millers* which contains stories that teach lessons on courtesy, health, and safety. After this break, we decided to return to rereading the Bible to help build on the foundations that were already in place.

The Children's Illustrated Bible (published by Star Song) has proven to be just what we needed. First, the stories are the right length for short attention spans and are illustrated with much attention to detail. Second, the maps in the book give us the ability to expand into the geography of biblical lands. My children are now learning facts about the Holy Land that I was ignorant of until I reached college age! We refer to the maps frequently and study the photos included in the text of things you would find during Jesus' time. Third, we make use of the Scripture verses in the side margin to give us verses to ponder. When we come upon these verses, the children look them up in their own Bibles. They are responsible for finding the verse themselves so that they can have the experience of rummaging through the pages in search of truth. This helps them to begin to master the use of the Bible. As a good friend of mine taught me, it is important to get Bibles into the hands of our children and teach them to use them.

Because Scripture memorization is so difficult for me personally, it can be difficult to enforce in my children. Because this is a weak area for me, I chose the option of using Steve Green's video and tape series "Hide 'Em in Your Heart," which introduces kids to important verses of the Bible. We also have worked to memorize hymns—a very worthwhile activity.

Because Michael has done a musical treatment of the entire Bible (*Ancient Faith* on the Old Testament, *The Life* on the life of Christ, *Present Reality* on the New Testament letters, and *Unveiled Hope* on the book of Revelation), we use his songs as reinforcement to a lesson. After reading about

Simeon in the Gospel of John, we listen to "Now that I've Held Him in My Arms" (from *The Early Works*/Benson)— or when reading about Isaac in Genesis we listen to "They Called Him Laughter" (from *The Beginning*/Sparrow). It really makes the stories come alive!

This year we are using an excellent book called *The Greenleaf Guide to Old Testament History* (published by Greenleaf Press). This study takes you through the Old Testament. We like this particular study guide because it supports our philosophy of studying history from a biblical worldview. It assists parents in studying the history of Israel, an important foundation for understanding the New Testament. It is part of a curriculum that we plan to follow for several years. This curriculum integrates great literature from the time period that you are studying.

Through the repetition of reading the Bible over and over with our children and building on the precepts it teaches, we can instill in them a thorough knowledge of the Bible. By reading devotional materials in combination with Scripture, we show them what living a life of obedience to the gospel looks like. And by teaching them songs, we give them a tool that allows them to express their response to what they have learned. Thus, prayerfully, we will attain our goal of training their listening ears to the voice of the Shepherd.

Listening to Your Life

Although the Bible is the primary way in which our children can hear the voice of the Shepherd, there are other ways that you can help them see glimpses of Jesus. The creation itself is a testimony. Very early in their lives our children become aware of all that is around them. When you express your animated delight over any aspect of nature that surrounds you, you are offering a form of praise and adoration for God's handiwork. Acknowledgment of His incredible work on this earth should become a habit. Just as the birds raise their spring chorus in the early morning hours, our homes should be filled with song. We hear His voice in the stories written for us, in His handiwork surrounding us, and in His love and compassion felt through the actual presence of our loved ones.

Sometimes it is through the presence of friends that we can best hear the Shepherd's voice. Three months after the birth of our third child, I became very ill with bronchitis. Sleep was my best friend, but with so much of it I would wake up disoriented. I wanted nothing more than the Lord's presence, but He seemed so far away. I suffered with the loneliness that often comes with serious illness. Lying there one morning, I heard the kitchen door opening and familiar voices floating up the stairs, accompanied by the clamoring of pots and pans. Soon the fragrant odor of soup reached me where I lay, and I listened to low voices chatting as they prepared the meal. I listened intently and recognized the voices of two of my dearest friends. In hearing their voices, I recognized His. He was with me, and He had sent them! I realized that day how much my family and friends meant and what a gift they were from God. They are representatives of His love and His continual reaching out. Have you not also heard His voice in the greeting of a friend?

As a child, though, it is probably in the familiar voice of our parents that we best sense the loving care of the Shepherd. If your love models for your children the love of God, what could be a more sensible decision than to school your children at home, where you can be with them, guiding and influencing them, preparing them to live for God in a godless world? It takes time and repetition to learn to walk. The walk of faith is no different. Homeschooling provides us with more time to put into the development of our children's character. Our talks can be more leisurely, and even the mundane activities of the day can be opportunities to talk, to impart a truth, or to witness a parable in the experiences of the day. When a day has not gone well, we have experienced it together. We can talk about it, understand it together, and pray that the next day might be better. I would not want to give up the many wonderful opportunities that homeschooling provides for helping me know my child more intimately.

Just as Michael and I would check handwriting for neatness or a report for accuracy, so we check the attitudes of our children for the sake of character building. This is one of those critical areas where I really believe that our goals can be better accomplished at home. Part of the reason for this is that training one's character involves exercising a special kind of authority and attentiveness that is just not possible in a large classroom. Ultimately, Michael and I want to be a part of this process. We enjoy the extra time homeschooling gives us with our children and the opportunity for getting to know them and their needs in the closest way possible.

Michael's Perspective
Making Christ the Center

"Therefore everyone who hears these words of mine and puts them into practice is like a wise man who built his house on the rock."

In Matthew, chapter 7, at the end of a lengthy teaching session, Jesus leaves His listeners with a wonderful image. It is not simply a picture of what wise people are supposed to do, but also a picture of what our lives will look like if we put Jesus' words into practice. It is more a lesson about listening and doing, than just simple common sense.

If homeschooling is about anything, it is about building foundations. It is about avoiding the sometimes shaky soil of public education and seeking out solid ground upon which to help our children construct their lives. It is about establishing a footing for them which is founded on the bedrock of the words of Jesus.

ll sounds well and good, but how does one go
omplishing such a goal? What does a teaching
system that is based on practicing Jesus' words look like?

Simply said (though not so simply done), it is a method
which places Christ at the center of all our understanding,
a methodology that we might call "Christocentric." Dietrich Bonhoeffer, a pastor who was martyred by the Nazis at
the end of World War II, laid out this approach in a small
but powerful book called *Christ the Center*. In this book, he
explained that even as everything should be brought under
submission to Christ, so also everything should be understood through Him.

What other approach to studying history is truly valid
except the one that understands the plan and purpose of
Christ which is woven into history? How else are we to
fully appreciate the various sciences which focus on creation until we first acknowledge that it was in fact through
Jesus that the universe came into being (John 1; Colossians
1; Hebrews 1)? What meaning is there in higher math and
physics apart from gaining an appreciation for the structure and order which are a genuine reflection of the Creator? And what else is philosophy for but to show us that
truth is woven into the fabric of creation by the One called
Truth?

Our family enjoys astronomy. We set up the telescope in
the front yard many nights to look more closely at the familiar face of the moon, or perhaps some nebula we've all
become acquainted with. Some nights we scan the surface
features of planets like Jupiter or Saturn. Often we just lie
on lawn chairs without the telescope and look for the outlines of constellations or the Milky Way, or perhaps even an
occasional meteorite. On sunny days we look for sunspots
with a special hydrogen-alpha filter. (You should never
look directly at the sun without special gear like this!)

But these nights together are not simply relaxing family
time. These sessions are intensely "informational." That is,
whenever we observe an object, we take the time to look it

up in one of our reference books. We find out how many years distant the object may be, and then sometimes look up in other sources to find out what was happening historically at the time the light left that nebula or star. If it is one of the astronomical objects mentioned in the Bible (the "cords of Orion" or the Pleiades, for example), we will examine that scriptural passage. We study the sky together as well as enjoy it.

Underneath all our involvement in astronomy is the understanding that this particular part of creation we revel in is, after all, the creation of God. We appreciate the stars as handiwork, as an "artful creation," as "poiema." The facts and figures are meant to enhance our appreciation and delight in the wonder of the beauty of all the Father has fashioned by His hand. Astronomy becomes doxology. We can approach anything we study in this same fashion.

The result of this method is what might be called "the circle of Christ-centeredness." Many times Susan and I have seen that whenever we center the teaching of any subject on Christ at the outset, the children inevitably respond, not with a reference to the subject at hand, but to Jesus Himself.

One night, Will and I stayed up late looking for meteors. With Susan, we had scaled the roof and sat there, bundled up against the cold, watching (with increasingly stiff necks) for streaks in the sky. I explained to Will that meteorites are tiny specks of dust which vaporize when they strike the atmosphere. We talked about a great meteor shower that was seen in the United States before the Civil War. It lead to a significant revival in our country, as many people initially thought it was the end of the world. I tried to make the most of the moment, explaining everything I knew about meteors.

We saw several that night, but Will always missed them, his attention attracted elsewhere. Susan and I would gasp with delight upon seeing one, but he was always looking the other way. He became frustrated to the point of tears and accused us of making up the whole thing. He had not seen a single one!

So I held him in my lap and placed his head in my hands so that he would have to look up. And then it happened. He saw his first meteorite!

We had begun the evening with a prayer of appreciation to God for the beauty of the night sky, for the peaceful quiet of the night, and for the chance to be together; we had centered the experience upon Christ. But what followed was at least an hour of facts and figures, dates and distances—hopefully interesting, but not remotely devotional. What was striking was Will's response when he saw the dazzling spectacle. "Thank You, Lord!" he shouted up into the dark face of the sky. He had learned that evening all the facts about meteors. He had also learned a difficult lesson about the necessity of patience during the long wait. But in the end it all came back to thanksgiving, even praise. Since the beautiful flash in the sky was the Lord's doing, who else should he thank?

"Therefore everyone who hears these words of mine," Jesus said. Teaching our children how to listen and be aware of these words in everything they read and see and experience, how to hear the sound of them even in the silence of the stars, will provide for them a Christ-centered foundation that will never fail them even in the most severe storm.

THREE

A Vision for Character

Day by day I write across
The pages of your life
Some sentences of kindness
And some paragraphs of light
May they be words of love and words
of hope
Not words of dark despair
For on your soul
The world will read them there

Lyric from "The Letter"/recorded by Steve Green
Words by Michael Card/Music by Phil Naish
Used by permission

I have asked Michael to take the lead in this chapter in an attempt to reflect God's order in our home. One of the unique responsibilities delegated to men is to keep their homes in order. One aspect of this is shaping, through love, the character of their wives and children. This direction from the head of our household is a provision that blankets us with wisdom and grace.

On the pages which follow, Michael shares his vision for character. This vision is the bedrock for building virtues such as peace, patience, humility, kindness, goodness, self-control, obedience, faithfulness, thankfulness, meekness, forgiveness and the greatest virtue of all . . . love.

Michael's Perspective

"Without a vision the people perish." Why should this be true? What is there about vision that protects us, nurtures us, and keeps us from death? Could it be that having a vision provides us with a course, a path which, if we keep to it, will keep us from getting lost? Or maybe vision is important in that it gives us some sense of what is truly valuable and what is not, so that we can keep clear of people and places which might endanger if not our very lives, at least the well-being of our souls.

When we decided to school our children at home, there was already a vision in place for our marriage. Perhaps it was that vision that led us to decide to homeschool in the first place. And nothing has tested the reality of that vision more than homeschooling—an arduous task for which Susan has borne so much of the burden. I'm happy to say that our vision remains intact, through all the struggles and difficulties which we face from day to day, because in its essence, it is a vision of Christ.

In Philippians 2:6-11 we find a wonderful passage of Scripture that was a hymn used in the worship services of the early church. Known as the "Carmen Christi" or "hymn to Christ," it is a song that first-century spies overheard the Christians singing at a time when the church was meeting in secret. It was a hymn which undoubtedly afforded them a measure of comfort in their trials because it offered a vision of who Christ was and what He had accomplished.

In this hymn, Jesus' incarnation is highlighted by its three central characteristics: servanthood, humility, and radical obedience. It is from this simple, ancient song that Susan and I derive our vision of who Jesus is and what He means to us. It is the vision that shapes our individual lives, our marriage, our family life, and even the way we choose to educate our children.

Servanthood

Who, being in very nature God, did not consider equality with God something to be grasped, but made himself nothing, taking the very nature of a servant, being made in human likeness. And being found in appearance as a man, he humbled himself and became obedient to death—even death on a cross! (Philippians 2:6-8).

"He came in the form of a servant," the hymn declares. What could have been more unlikely than that the King of the universe would have chosen to demonstrate the fullness of His love by becoming a servant?

In reading the Gospels we are struck by the fact that Jesus is as much a butler to the disciples as He is their Lord. We find Him again and again reaching out to serve them. When they are tired, He is sensitive to their needs and takes them aside to rest. When they are hungry, He feeds them. At the Last Supper, He takes a basin and towel in hand and washes their feet. Even after the resurrection, in John chapter 21, Jesus stands on the shore to meet the tired and disheartened disciples. He waits there, with scars on His hands and feet, not as much to be worshiped by them as to prepare breakfast for them. He is their Servant/Savior. It is the shape of His life.

When we turn our thoughts to homeschooling, to molding the hearts of our children, this vision of Jesus as Servant provides the foundation for a biblical value system. What is more valuable: to be served or to serve? Our children will readily answer (whether they have yet come to fully internalize it or not) that they have chosen to be servants. They know the command of Jesus: "Whoever would be great among you must become a servant."

Humility

Sung to a melody long lost, the "Carmen Christi" tells us that Jesus "made Himself nothing." What other character trait is as undeniable in the life of Jesus as His humility? Though He might have grasped equality with God, He chose instead to be a humble servant. Most often when He performed a miracle He would direct the thanksgiving to the Father. "I can do nothing without the Father," Jesus would say.

In our own time we have lost sight of this true form of humility. At best we can offer a cheap imitation, a false modesty. "That was a good concert," someone will say to me.

"Oh no," I inevitably moan, "I sang flat, my guitar was out of tune . . ." This passes for humility in the minds of many. In fact, it is only a disguised form of pride, a ploy to hear more compliments and assurances. How different is true humility!

True humility is nothing more or less than knowing who we are in Christ. Only relationship with Him can give us the genuine article. On the one hand He convicts us of our sin and fallenness, telling us our righteousness is only "filthy rags." And then in the next breath He smothers us with affection, as the father did for his prodigal son, telling us how much we are valued, that He loves us so much that He would rather die than live without us.

That is who I am. That is who you are if you know Him. We are men and women, boys and girls, who are truly hopeless yet full of hope, truly lost but nonetheless truly found. In His embrace there is no room for either false humility or pride.

As our children grow, trying to piece together the puzzle of their own identity, we hope to provide this vision of who they truly are—a picture unaffected by either peer pressure or a warped value system that would tell them anything more or less.

Obedience

He was "obedient to death," the song tells us. "Even death on a cross." Such a level of obedience can be called nothing less than radical. In the Garden of Gethsemane we see Jesus struggling with His will versus the will of the Father. Part of Him simply does not want to make this ultimate sacrifice. In essence He says, "If there is any way this cup can pass, if there is any way You can get me out of this, do it!" That human part of Jesus, knowing everything that lurked in the darkness before Him, knew that this was not what He wanted. What else could "nevertheless not *My* will but *Thine* be done" mean if not that there was a genuine struggle between the two wills there in the garden? So the heart of the victory that was won on the cross of Jesus has to do with radical obedience. Not with doing what you already want to do, but in doing the very last thing that you would want to do!

In our world today, obedience seems to be a lost virtue. Parents often try to shape the world in such a way that it suits their children's wills. Then obedience is not even an issue! Bedtimes are flexible, as are meals. Chores are whittled away to meaningless tasks that can be done in a few minutes. We try not to make them do what they don't want to do (which would teach them true obedience), but find those things that they are already predisposed toward and then make our requests accordingly.

Is it any wonder that employers are clamoring for employees who will carry out simple requests? That the military is quickly becoming an advanced day-care system? That colleges cannot find enough students who will simply show up regularly for class? We are facing a generation of young people who simply cannot understand why they should have to do something they do not want to do—anything that might interfere with their pursuit of pleasure.

What might have seemed in the beginning to be a gift of freedom to our children has become the worst kind of enslavement to self. Many of them are waking up from what they thought was a dream and discovering through broken marriages (Why should I obey my vows if I don't want to?), spoiled academic careers, and an endless procession of dead-end jobs, that they were betrayed by parents who simply lacked the courage to say "no" to them.

The only hope for our children (and our culture as well) is to reclaim a Christ-centered vision for them. A vision that teaches them the value and imperative of serving others. A vision that tells them who they are: dearly loved children of the Father. A vision that frees them from slavery to self by teaching them obedience to the will of God. This is the heart of the vision that Susan and I share for our children.

Susan's Perspective
Implementing the Vision

It is easier to talk about issues like servanthood, humility, and obedience than it is to make them a reality in the lives of our children. We know that it is not enough for us to memorize the meaning of these words; we must live them out in our actions. It can be difficult to teach these qualities when we know that we are in our own lives still struggling to learn these Christlike qualities. As parents, we may lack the confidence to teach characteristics that we know we fail to carry out as we should, or we fear that we will be exposed as hypocrites in the eyes of our children. But we must remember that it is only by the Lord's grace that we are qualified to be His representatives and to bear the responsibility of training our children in His likeness. If we abandon this vision because of our fear, then we are left to wander aimlessly with no direction other than our own self-interest. It is far better that we admit our frequent failings and still keep our eyes focused on the race we are called to run.

The characteristics which Michael alluded to out of Philippians chapter 2 seem to me to be closely intertwined. They are not so much three separate characteristics as they are three aspects of a single, unified attitude. Without humility, how can you have the heart of a servant? Or a heart of obedience? Humility is the key characteristic that makes servanthood and obedience realities. It is where we must start in order to adopt a life of Christlike servanthood and radical obedience.

Humility is not taught; it is caught. I cannot teach my children to be humble, but I can have them participate in activities that are humbling in nature—activities like cleaning up after their brother or sister. I can also help identify and hold them accountable for evidences of pride which might be taking root in their young lives, for pride is the very antithesis of humility.

Pride shows itself in a number of ways: simple comments made about other people in a critical, self-uplifting way; the subtle nuances of tone between siblings that give clues that one considers himself or herself better than the other; a competitive spirit that expresses itself through a haughtiness and a snubbing of potential opponents. There are also nonverbal clues, expressions that let you know that your child has climbed the pedestal and needs to come down before he or she falls.

At the core of servanthood and obedience is the attitude of humility. It is a vital component in godly character, and its presence or absence can be clearly seen in the way we live our lives.

Of course we know that obedience is doing what we are told. But as believers we must go a step further. We must not only do as we are asked, but also do it with a good attitude. Sometimes it will take some time to fully reconcile ourselves to what we must do out of obedience, but we must strive not only to obey, but to obey with the right attitude. Obedience is an absolute requirement for those who would be servants.

Servants in Action

A servant is one who brings aid, who helps, serves, meets needs. Our service is ultimately to the Lord, but obedience to Him means that we will serve others. I see service to others as falling into three basic categories: service to immediate family members, service to extended family and friends, and service to the community.

When it comes to serving family members, we may assume that this is a lesson we have already taught very well. We can delude ourselves into thinking that just because we have given a long list of verbal directives that we have taught our children to serve one another:

"Help your sister with that."
"You need to share that with your brother."
"C'mon, take some initiative to involve the little ones
    in what you're doing."

But such commands do not exhaust the lessons our children must learn about serving one another. I am continually being reminded that teaching important truths is a time-consuming pursuit that involves long-term dedication to the task. These important lessons are not easy to learn. The words must be followed up with actions!

One activity that I have found useful in helping my children see the heart of servanthood is to have them clean the room of a sibling or take over a chore that the other one normally performs. There is always a moment of stunned silence when they realize what it is that I have just asked them to do! "But . . ." they implore. I am quick to cut off their complaints and explain simply that they need to learn to serve one another. "No grumbling," I always warn.

During this exercise I am always close at hand observing them. I keep my eye out for two things: First, what is their attitude while making their brother or sister's bed? Are they doing it carelessly or with thoughtfulness? Are they being sensitive to where the toys and books belong, or are they just tossing things onto the most convenient shelves? I point out to them what I see. Sometimes, by copying their actions and mimicking their voice, I will demonstrate the difference between serving with love and serving with spite. (Okay, I admit it. We do tend to get a bit dramatic in our home!)

Second, when they return to their own rooms, I observe how gracious they are about being served. Perhaps things are not always done exactly as they would have preferred. Do they grumble about what their brother or sister did? Or do they thank them? I hold them accountable on this point. They should be grateful, not critical, for all the work their sibling put into cleaning their room. This simple exercise alone can take the better part of a morning, but it is time well spent.

Sometimes, for effect, I will use the word *serve* in giving instructions to the children. Recently, I asked Katie to make some chocolate milk for Will and carry it to him. She huffed about it. "Come here," I said. "Here is the milk and the chocolate. Serve your brother." The look on her face changed as she gained a different perspective on the action she was being asked to perform. By using the word *serve*, I was employing a word that is uncharacteristic of our usual vocabulary. Instead of just saying, "Take this to your brother," we have put the request on a completely different level and couched it in a language that she immediately recognizes as spiritual. I am no longer telling her to passively obey, but to take an active role in the process and serve her brother.

When I think of service to extended family and friends, I think of letters, phone calls, and basic hospitality. Letters and phone calls can communicate thankfulness, encouragement, sorrow, or whatever else we feel. They are a basic expression of love and caring. Letters have a way of making us feel really special. For a brief moment we have become the 'chosen' one. Someone has taken the time and put forth the effort to communicate especially with us. Hospitality is a very concrete form of servanthood. It is making the person who is visiting feel cared for. Will recently had a friend over, who arrived just as Will was sitting down to lunch. I discreetly reminded him, "Take care of your friend while he is here." That's all it took to get Will "minding after" his little buddy: fixing him a drink, offering him a sandwich, and asking him what he would like to do first. It has taken some time to teach this lesson, but in one brief moment I felt the satisfaction of a lesson well learned.

Service to our community can take many forms. For us, it can be as small as offering encouragement to our office staff or as large as participating in a community outreach.

One of the things we have committed to this year is tutoring. Once a week we meet with inner-city children for an hour and a half. This form of community service was made available through our church's outreach program. This year we have had three children assigned to us. We help them with their homework and work on areas that their school teachers have indicated are weak. For one child Katie brings a storybook so she and the little girl can alternate reading to one another. Will participates in flashcard drills or Math Safari with the two boys. Both Katie and Will have seen servanthood in action and have also broadened their horizons by making new friends.

Of course we must weigh all our choices carefully, keeping in mind what the needs of our family are and not letting community service interfere with what we need to cover in school. But I know of other homeschool families who perform secret forms of encouragement for the church staff, visit nursing homes, or help in soup kitchens. Whatever the deed may be, seeing us serve others helps our children to extend the concept of servanthood beyond their family and friends and into a fallen world. Acts of love and compassion are demonstrations that speak as clearly as the words "I love you" spoken aloud.

Beyond Recognition

Not only must we teach our children the important lessons discussed above, but we must also help them get beyond the need to always receive recognition for their good deeds. As they grow into adulthood, how wonderful if they have learned the joy of doing acts of kindness in secret, where it is only the heavenly Father who knows what they have done. I praise my children freely for the good behavior and attitudes I see in them. I know they hunger for this recognition. But I have also tried to encourage them often to do something nice that no one else knows about. Although it seems that they always end up sharing the secret with me, this seems to come more from the fun of sharing a secret than from a desire for affirmation for what they have done!

The issue of service has been key to Michael and me for years, and we have emphasized it in a myriad of ways. I know that we are not always perfect examples and that sometimes our attempts to explain our vision only garner blank stares from the children, but we never tire of helping them to see that Christlikeness involves humility and service. To obey is not only an action, but also an attitude. This is the vision we share with our children, the driving force that keeps us on the path to growth.

Four

A Walk with Creativity

There's a way that a child
Can look at the world
And see through the eyes of the heart
They see meaning beyond the mystery
Hear the silence of the stars

So close your eyes so you can see
The way He meant this world to be
And understand with childlike heart
The place we end is where we start

Lyric from "Close Your Eyes So You Can See"
Words and Music by Michael Card
Used by permission

"Mom?"

A feeble, trembling voice reached my ears as I was awakened with a sudden start.

"Mom?" The voice whispered again, this time with more urgency. I recognized the voice as belonging to my son Will. Sitting up in bed, I reached through the darkness, stretching my hand toward a faint silhouette.

"Will! What's wrong?" I asked as I pulled the motion-less shadow toward me.

"Mom, I have something to tell you." He spoke with that quiet confessional tone which usually meant, "I have done something wrong but take pity on me."

"It's this," he continued. "Katie said I could sleep in her bed tonight. And while we were waiting to fall asleep, I started to tell her stories about monsters that would scare her. Well, she asked me to stop." He hesitated. "But I thought of one more really good one, and as I was telling her . . . I scared myself! Can I sleep in your bed tonight?"

Will, who was only six years old at the time of this story, has been gifted with a vivid imagination—one that brings pleasure and insight during the day, but also has the potential to plague him at night. During daylight hours it manifests itself in the form of detailed drawings that are reflective of a true artist's touch and an artist's mind. He does not usually draw by copying from the pictures of others or even by painstakingly studying still objects. Instead, every drawing is an original idea coming from within his own imagination. This is great when it comes to the mental images he experiences during the day, the ones he so carefully shapes into striking pictures. However, at bedtime they can take on a different nature, stronger in intensity and definition, sometimes frightening. Darkness has a way of making us fear what may be lurking in its shadows.

By the time he had reached four years of age, we realized that Will had a special artistic gift. Up to that time, I had always provided plenty of crayons, markers, and paper. But for some reason they were seldom used, leaving me wondering why my children did not enjoy drawing or coloring. After all, how could one resist a new box of Crayola crayons? Katie could not tolerate the lack of perfection in her drawings, so she abandoned any attempt to be creative in this area unless I prodded and pushed. Will was simply not very interested in finding creative outlets, until one day our friend Ms. Pat gave him a dinosaur coloring book.

On that particular afternoon, I was surprised to see him sitting on top of the dining room table, leaning over a coloring book completely surrounded by crayons. "Will," I exclaimed, "you're coloring!" I stopped what I was doing to marvel at his work.

"Yep," he replied without looking up. He spent nearly four hours hunched over his coloring book, taking only a couple short breaks. I did not dare interrupt for fear of breaking his concentration. That was a turning point. He spent time coloring almost every day until he eventually abandoned the coloring books and began drawing primitive pictures of dinosaurs. By the time he was five, he began drawing dragons and other mysterious reptilian creatures. He even made the loveliest garden of "monster flowers" to hang behind my bed when I returned home from the hospital with his baby brother.

What we found particularly interesting about Will's newfound love for drawing was the necessity of doing it. Not a day would go by without him asking for paper and pencils, his mind intent on his purpose. "Mom, I have to go draw." And off he would go, lost in thought. The resulting pictures made it evident that his ability was superior not to just that of other children his age, but to that of most adults as well. Michael and I responded by providing supplies, time, and encouragement. For Christmas, Michael built him a drawing desk with a lamp and swivel chair that he uses to this day.

One thing which impressed us from the start was the originality of his work. He illustrated stories which took place in different worlds—worlds inhabited by strange and unique creatures. He eventually focused on dragons and spent an entire year perfecting every detail. I still have large pieces of paper with a single attempt at an eye, tooth, or claw. The heads of his dragons were drawn with a three-quarter twist to give a three-dimensional appearance—something he learned to do without instruction. These innovations required diligence on Will's part, and the availability of pencils and paper.

One evening while he was working on a new sketch, Michael and I went to his room to see what he was conjuring up. We peered over his shoulder and were delighted by an amazing drawing, knowing that we were certainly not capable of such fine work.

Michael leaned over to catch his attention. "Will, where do all these ideas come from?"

Will responded simply, still continuing in his work, "From my imagination."

Fascinated, Michael asked him, "What does your imagination look like?"

"Well," he said very seriously, "it looks like a cloud. And in the cloud is a heart. And Dad, sometimes the Lord looks over my shoulder, and He helps me to draw." What precious insight from a six-year-old, and what a privilege for us to be able to share it with him.

What Is Imagination?

Will understands that the imagination is the place where his ideas come from. For him, it exists in the form of a cloud with a heart in it. Most of us have not taken the time to consider what our imagination is, despite the fact that we use it every day. To use the imagination is to form a mental image of something. The image can be real or it can be make-believe. You can imagine new experiences or recall experiences from the past. You can even travel to places that do not exist at all. The imagination is one of the most mysterious and yet powerful tools the Lord has provided us with. But what makes it important?

In Matthew 13:10, the frustrated disciples asked Jesus, "Why do you speak to the people in parables?" In verses 13 and 14 Jesus replies, "This is why I speak to them in parables: Though seeing, they do not see; though hearing, they do not hear or understand. In them is fulfilled the prophecy of Isaiah: 'You will be ever hearing but never understanding; you will be ever seeing but never perceiving.'"

Jesus tells His disciples that the vital key for "seeing" and "hearing," for understanding and perceiving, is the imagination. Jesus Himself used parables to engage the imagination of the disciples. These parables continue to speak to our imaginations today. By telling stories, He spoke to our visual minds so that we could "see" pictures of what He was trying to teach. His consistency in using this method of teaching shows the importance that Jesus placed on using the imagination. It was His favorite tool— one He used to reach into our hearts. What do you see when you read these words of Jesus: "A farmer went out to sow his seed. As he was scattering the seed . . ." (Matthew 13:3,4)?

Michael has been grappling for over five years with a way to explain the creative process and how it relates to our faith. He taught a Bible college course entitled "Christ and the Creative Process," which helped him to understand the imagination more clearly as he taught students and interacted with them. While he was preparing for the classes, he would share new insights during walks we would take together. During one of these walks he shared with me a definition he had come to. "I realize now what the imagination is and why Jesus used parables to teach. The imagination is the bridge between the heart and mind."

Michael's definition helped me understand more clearly that the imagination is important because it serves as the gateway to understanding. To really have an impact on the hearts of our children, we must reach their minds. The reverse is true as well: To reach their minds, we must engage their hearts. This takes some creative effort on the part of the teacher and parent, putting forth the kind of effort that Jesus did on our behalf.

Posting Guard

If it is true that our hearts can be reached through our minds, and that our imagination serves as a gateway to understanding, then we, as parents, must teach our children to "post guard." As eager as we are to have truth take root in our children, foolishness and lies have access through that same gate of imagination. To police the entry, parents and children must become disciplined in guarding their hearts and minds.

Keeping children at home for their education, especially during the elementary grades, can provide a protective environment to train them in the discipline of discernment. That is, training them to recognize good and moral behavior versus foolish and potentially bad behavior. Even children with a strong Christian background need this continued training in discipline, because they cannot

help but be influenced by the decline in morality that has swept our culture.

We all have a tendency to become desensitized by the behavior of those around us and to adapt to their value systems. The Bible refers to this process of desensitizing as "the hardening of the heart," and we are potential victims of this spiritual state unless we learn to "post a guard" over our hearts.

We have had to learn to help Will post a guard in the area of his creativity. Will loves to draw dragons. Because of that, he likes to look at the pictures of dragons that others have drawn. He enjoys illustrations that depict all kinds of these mystical beasts. Stories like *The Reluctant Dragon,* or *St. George and the Dragon,* or Ruth Stiles Gannett's trilogy that begins with *My Father's Dragon* are all good, captivating stories that keep our imaginations within the boundaries of wholesomeness. But not all dragons are harmless fictional creatures. Fascination with dragons has the potential to become a negative influence. On occasion, Michael and I have had to point out to Will how the eyes in some illustrations looked evil and the composition of the artwork was scary. Basically, they were something he did not need to see. He would argue, "But I am not afraid of that!"

So would begin a discussion on the fact that what may appear harmless during the day may terrify him at night. Besides, we told him, there are certain paths we do not need to meander down. Evil is one of them.

We defined a boundary for him that he should try to keep from crossing. And this includes his own drawings. If he thinks they would scare his baby brother, then he knows his drawing may be too mean or violent. He has learned to make an adjustment, sometimes by simply softening the look of the eyes. To help protect Will in this area of potential problems, we are careful with what we make available to him, such as books, videos, or toys. Although we have made a few mistakes, we try to keep inappropriate material banned from the privilege of influencing his mind. As Paul instructs us in the letter to the Philippians:

> Finally, brothers, whatever is true, whatever is noble, whatever is right, whatever is pure, whatever is lovely, whatever is admirable—if anything is excellent or praiseworthy—think about such things (Philippians 4:8).

This powerful tool called the imagination is the gateway to our innocence. Once innocence is lost, it is lost forever. When we reflect on our own childhood, we can remember the preciousness of being free from the encumbrances of the world and the dark lessons of reality it offered. Even a brief television preview can rob our children of a portion of that innocence. Or the news, set up to serve us by "keeping us informed," can rob our children of their innocence by introducing topics they are not mature enough to grasp. They really do not need to be exposed to the great evils of our culture at such a young age, before they are mature enough to handle such disturbing realities as murder, rape, and abortion. I do not let them watch the nightly news for fear of introducing them to issues they are too young to be able to face.

Like etching a design on glass, these visual images etch themselves deeply into our minds. We can never be too careful with protecting our children from what their eyes see or what their ears hear. Striving to protect their innocence does not, as some suggest, keep them culturally illiterate. Instead, it is the wisdom of knowing how much they can really handle and how soon. Our purpose in protecting them is to prepare them adequately to face the hard issues that lie ahead. The Lord equips us with armor (Ephesians 6:11) to endure trials and tribulations. By keeping a clear image of what is good and right, and by us training them to listen for the Shepherd's voice, our children will be better prepared to face the battles in the long life that awaits them.

The Source of Creativity

Imagination is the source of creativity. Creativity is the ability to conceive ideas and communicate them to others in unique ways. It is awe-inspiring to see how creativity works. For example, I can be standing in front of a bolt of fabric in my local "Stitcher's Garden" shop and can imagine in two seconds what will actually take me an entire day to make. In my mind, I have cut the fabric, sewn it, and even added some contrasting piping to the collar of a dress for Maggie. It looks so beautiful in my mind's eye that I buy the fabric then and there, determined to go home and create a dress. Once the dress is completed, my creative exploit is finished and I benefit from the pleasure of seeing my little girl romping around in something I made. The dress that my daughter wears is a product of my creativity, but before it could be made, it first had to be "imagined."

But where did this creativity come from? What motivates me to pull out my watercolors during the spring season in an attempt to paint the flower of a peony bush? What makes me fuss over the table settings or write in my journal? Edith Schaeffer answered this question for me years ago. In her book *The Hidden Art of Homemaking*, she validated and encouraged this "fever" called creativity. At one time I thought it was somehow not right that I needed to express myself in impulsive and bold displays of my creative desire. I thought that maybe this was a weakness in my spiritual life. "But," as Edith says of her own awakening to creativity, "the heart of the discovery is this: we are created in the likeness of the Creator. We are created in the image of a Creator."[1] In other words, I cannot help but be creative because I am made in the image of God, who is "the First Artist." We are all made in His image, both parents and children, and we are made to respond to Him and to each other in creative ways.

Creativity Is All Around Us

It seems to be easier for adults to see creative expression in children than in themselves. I am frequently surprised to hear friends make comments like, "I don't have a creative bone in my body." I always respond in firm disagreement and begin illustrating for them the creative elements I see in their life. From the way knickknacks are arranged on a display shelf, to how a garden is laid out, to the color chosen for this year's file folders, to the bandanna chosen at the last minute to tie in the hair, all these require someone to make a choice in shaping, designing, or coloring to suit his or her concept of beauty. Creativity abounds! We must learn to recognize it in our daily lives, allowing it to color our hearts and minds with joy. Remember, we serve a creative God who takes delight in our reflection of His image, the image of creativity.

Play

Maggie and I were playing with bubbles one day in our "schoolroom." I was blowing bubbles, and she was trying to catch them. Will walked in. He did not say a word to either of us as he crossed the room to join in our play. His interpretation of what we were playing was not at all like mine. "Kooshshshshsh!" was his first comment as his hands swept through the air.

---

1. *The Hidden Art of Homemaking*, Tyndale House Publishers, Edith Schaeffer, pg. 24 (1971).

"Oh no! Maggie! The spaceship!" he exclaimed as he pointed to the luminous light fixture that hung low overhead. "It's sending enemy aircraft down to destroy the planet! We must save it!"

"Save it!" Maggie parroted, and they began war on the spherical aircrafts that floated through the air.

The war ended for him almost as quickly as it had started. "Mom, can I go have a snack?" When he left to get his snack, he left behind a two-year-old sparked by imaginative play.

When Katie's best friend Jessica comes over for the afternoon, they always enact the same ritual upon her arrival. Screaming with delight at the sight of one another, they race upstairs to the closet where costumes and spare dresses are kept and begin one of many changes in clothing. The afternoon just wouldn't be right if they stayed in normal clothes. After all, the costume must fit the character they are playing, and they do indeed have quite a repertoire. That is how they spend most of their time together,

contentedly changing costumes until Michael, with a dragon mask on, storms the castle and chases the princesses down the hall to the dragon's lair where they become his prisoners!

At the beginning of spring, when the dirt arrives for the garden beds, it sits behind the house waiting to be spread. Nathan could not be happier. His time and attention are completely absorbed by this mound of soil. He spends hours laboring in the warm sunshine, digging holes and sliding off mountains. When Will arrives on the scene, Nathan begins sliding off "the steepest cliff known to mankind." Only his brother's superhero strength can save him now! They stretch out their arms. The grasp for safety avoids the grave danger that is only inches away. In one nail-biting moment, Nathan is saved from his peril and can now resume his task of building truck beds. Every boy needs a dirt pile. This accessible resource quite simply brings out the best in their creative play.

I could give endless examples of creativity in play which are a delight to watch, as well as participate in. One of my best friends can be found in her daughter's playhouse assuming the role of Loreen, the Southern hairdresser with too much time on her hands. This kind of creative play can become contagious, as indeed it should. We, as parents, need to be participants in play, not only for the sake of our children, but also so that we do not lose touch with our childlikeness. As Jesus encourages us, "I tell you the truth, anyone who will not receive the kingdom of God like a little child will never enter it" (Luke 18:17). How like Jesus, to encourage us to play!

Arts and Crafts

Crayons and markers, glue and scissors, paper and tape, strings and boxes, are all resources that come to mind when thinking about arts and crafts. An endless variety of projects can be constructed out of very simple raw materials. Conceptualizing an idea is often the hardest part, but creativity is natural to children if they are given the supplies, the time, and some limited supervision.

Art projects are great for enhancing lessons or emphasizing a holiday. Because time is always a precious commodity in our household, I search through books for creative new ideas and occasionally will buy kits because of their convenience and how much energy they save me. We usually design our activities around events on the calendar or themes from our daily lessons. By doing it this way, I do not feel overwhelmed with the necessity of developing fresh ideas.

Frequently, I respond to the children's initiative and deviate from the plan. If they have a desire or interest, I encourage them to take the lead. Katie was interested in working with beads, so for her birthday we learned how to make bead bracelets. The hardest part of this project was following the pattern, but it was a great math exercise in learning how to use a graph, as well as a creative outlet. I can personally testify to the fact that the greatest motivating force for children is their own particular interests. I have learned that it is sometimes necessary to pull back and let their interests guide them. When I do that, I do not have to work nearly as hard in motivating them. They work hard because they want to!

For many children, drawing is intimidating and proves to be a stumbling block. They can become frustrated when their own drawings do not measure up to those in books. This was an extremely difficult area for Katie. But by giving her time (which amounted to four years) and consistent encouragement, we were able to help her overcome her frustrations and begin to enjoy drawing.

One tool which helped us immensely was a drawing and handwriting course for children called *Draw—Write—Now* by Marie Hablitzel and Kim Stitzer. This book provided Katie with the step stool she needed to reach a higher level of confidence. Most books will advise you against using symbols for drawing. Instead they encourage you to draw what you see. This approach simply frustrated Katie and closed off the possibility of ever finding freedom in drawing. My goal with Katie was to release her from being bound by intimidation, and this series of books helped accomplish this. She became confident almost overnight. The icing on the cake for us was the initiative that followed. She began bringing me pictures that she had drawn and colored. She even drew pictures for her friends. This was a great accomplishment because previously she would not have dared to try. The light in her eyes as she took her pencil in hand and her own satisfaction in her finished work was definitely worth the wait. While it took her longer to find her way, and though we traveled down a different path than that of her brother, we have arrived. She is now equipped with the confidence needed to explore this creative activity.

Drama and Storytelling

When it came to putting on a play for the first time, we underestimated what was required of us. While the children were energized, we became exhausted. What motivated me and the three other mothers involved was how sensible the idea was. We had all studied the 1700s with our children and had read all the Felicity books in the American Girls series. It seemed natural to want to do the creative thing and put on a play. After all, we thought, the theater kit would make it simple. All we had to do was follow the directions. Well, it was quite a bit more complicated than that, but it was certainly worth the effort it required!

What we did not realize was that we had our own creative inclinations to deal with while reading these simple directions. How, we asked ourselves, could we re-create this story in the most realistic way with the resources available? We began by asking our church's well-known and much-loved drama couple to teach a brief seminar. Charlie and Ruth Jones, known more familiarly by their stage name, "Peculiar People," generously gave hours of their time to coach the children in the fundamentals of acting. The children had to audition for their parts. They were taught exercises to relieve them of the jitters. They learned how to project their voices, how to block a play, and how to get into character. This was a wonderful experience in using the gifted people from our own community.

Each family had outside responsibilities. There were costumes to make, bulletins to print, refreshments to plan for, stage props to provide, and rehearsals to coach. On top of the regular demands of their studies, the children had high self-motivation to take the extra time to learn their parts well. By the end of second semester, they were ready to perform.

Of course it does not take a full-blown play to benefit from drama. An informal exercise in drama that can reap rich rewards is storytelling. This can be done very simply by reading stories aloud, with each child and adult taking a character. We read all of our read-alouds this way. Nathan, who is only four, read a book to me last night for the first time, but he already knows that changing his voice for the different characters makes the story more enjoyable to the listener. This is a wonderful exercise for everyone. Reading becomes interactive because the reader has to decide what the character is thinking and feeling. Different accents or voice intonations can be used to make the characters more interesting. Many nights you can find the Card family acting out a story from a book with a great deal of enjoyment and laughter.

Creativity and Development

The purpose of creativity, first and foremost, is to fulfill a part of God's purpose in creating us in His image. We reflect God's image by using our creative gifts to express ourselves. Our expression exposes who we are, our unique individuality. By showing the world our uniqueness, we bring glory to God by showing His greatness through the diversity of His creation. Diversity is not limited to the variety of different cultures, but is seen in every human being. Creativity is our voice telling our friends, families, and communities who we are.

From a more fundamental perspective, creativity is important for the proper development of our children. There are profound insights to be gained from looking at the developmental tasks defined by psychoanalyst E. H. Erikson, who has written of the stages children go through as they grow to become adults. One of these stages, "initiative versus guilt," can be related to learning to be creative. Initiative is learning to act out an idea without being urged or coerced. This is a valuable characteristic, but one that requires careful training. "Whether the child leaves this stage with his sense of initiative far outweighing his sense of guilt depends largely on how parents respond to his self-initiated activities."[2] Activities such as play and arts and crafts reinforce our children's sense of personal initiative. Nurturing children through this phase of their young life demands a lot of self-awareness on the part of the parents. Did I cut them off when they asked a question? Did they feel shamed for attempting something? Am I allowing them to try and sometimes fail? These are the kind of questions I must ask myself during the course of a day.

Nurturing a sense of personal initiative can be done through play. Children use large motor skills to explore their world through activities such as running, riding bikes, jumping rope, and other playground games. Fine motor skills are developed through activities like arts and crafts, music, and sewing. If given encouragement in these areas, children are more confident and more apt to try new challenges. If reprimanded too severely for failure in these areas, their sense of guilt and failure takes over and they grow up insecure, less likely to have the confidence to attempt new situations on their own.

Of course there is a balance here. Too much initiative in the hands of a preschooler can be difficult to handle at times, or sometimes just plain dangerous. Some expressions of initiative require adult supervision. Michael remembers when he was four years old and decided to make breakfast for everyone. He toasted a whole loaf of bread and spread the slices with peanut butter. His mother praised his intentions but encouraged his efforts in another

---

2. *Nursing Care of the Growing Family*, Adele Pilliteri, Little, Brown and Company, Boston, pg. 26 (1977).

direction. "Thanks, but no thanks" is a typical response to little helping hands.

Drama, storytelling, and music are all expressive activities that help in developing confidence, poise, narration, and courage. By participating in these kinds of things at a young age, children become less self-conscious in front of people. Their minds are rightfully preoccupied with articulating a thought or a part in a play, rather than being consumed with worry over the fact that they are being watched. One of our goals as a homeschooling community should be to raise leaders. Leaders need to be able to communicate confidently and well. Sometimes simple, playful activities can provide a wonderful foundation for future formalities.

All of us are encouraged by creative elements in our world. Life is very much a canvas awaiting our brushes. We may dip them in paint, or we may use musical notes, or we may be listeners who simply encourage and appreciate. We need to make our mark, whatever medium or role we choose. By expressing ourselves and encouraging our children to do the same, we serve the Lord faithfully by reflecting His image. We also serve our families and communities by enhancing their lives with a sign of our unique presence.

Providing the Tools

For creativity to bear its full fruit, we need to provide our children with the tools to use as they let their imaginations run wild. Having the necessary supplies around our home is one of the best ways to encourage their creativity. We try to tailor our stockpile of supplies to fit our children's interests. At the time I am writing this book, we have two preschoolers. One is getting a fresh pile of dirt as we face the summer months, and the other will be getting the hand-me-down easel for painting. Will is becoming interested in sculpting, so his grandmother gave him her leftover clay.

Katie is interested in making necklaces and bracelets, so she has been provided with a supply of beads. Besides providing special tools that encourage specific interests, we keep a few standard items on hand.

For arts and crafts we keep a stock of pens, pencils, color pencils, pastel pencils, paper, glue sticks, stamps and ink pads, blank note cards and envelopes, rolls of freezer paper, and a box of odds and ends like thread, string, ribbon, paper clips, pipe cleaners, and empty spools. We also have art books nearby if someone wants an idea. For painting we use acrylic paints and watercolors, large and small paintbrushes, and sponges that are cut in several different shapes. These items can be purchased inexpensively and have supplied our children with untold hours of creative entertainment.

We like to buy or make costumes from time to time. If I do not have the time to make something, I can always find cheap costumes after Halloween. (We try to be careful with our choice of costumes, as with anything else.) These come in handy for drama, storytelling, or playtime. Katie frequently goes to my sewing room and finds a large strip of leftover fabric. She can spend a whole afternoon working with that piece of fabric. The children have collected several puppets over the course of years, so one Christmas, Michael and I built a puppet theater for them. These are just a couple examples of the kinds of supplies that encourage the imagination through drama.

As for music, our piano is always available to the kids. Beyond that, we have our voices. Limiting the choices of what is available to listen to has been very helpful to my children, as well as myself. It focuses and concentrates our efforts into fewer areas. Often simplicity has great advantages over overwhelming variety for younger children. As they get older they will have the capacity to enjoy more variety. We keep a stereo in the classroom for the convenience of listening to tapes and stories.

Carefully chosen videotapes can also be very stimulating for children with a bent toward drama, art, and music, so I use them to supplement our lessons whenever appropriate. Educational toys that encourage imaginative play can be great resources. By providing the right tools for the children, I have gone a long way toward accomplishing my goal of encouraging their creativity. I have been constantly amazed at how little supervision my children need when they play creatively.

Making the Time, Making the Space

One of the best things about teaching at home is that it gives you the ability to tailor your time to suit the needs of you and your children. Creativity requires time and space. When Michael is writing an album or a book, he is always seeking large blocks of uninterrupted time. I found them essential as I wrote the book you are reading. Interruptions can break into your concentration and focus, because creating original work is an exhausting process of trial and error that requires time and space.

Our children require time without interruption as well. If I had put Will in kindergarten, I have no doubt the development of his gift would not be as far along as it is today. He would not have had the freedom to go on imaginative explorations with pen and paper because the structure of the public school day would probably have interrupted his thoughts and ideas. Structure works well with Katie and Nathan, but somehow it confines Will, with the result being that his motivation to learn begins to suffer.

When I talk about "providing space," I am referring to two situations. First, the physical area needs to be sufficient to work in. Maybe a tabletop, a desk, or an area within a room. Sometimes we spread freezer paper the entire length of the six-foot table in the schoolroom. I secure it with tape and put a fresh box of markers on top. Other times I let the children have at it with sponges and paints. They enjoy being able to stretch out their creative efforts over a seemingly unlimited space.

Space also refers to privacy. I try to provide Katie with quiet time so she can practice the piano without interruptions. It is her time to work unencumbered by younger siblings who want to join in. Will can draw anytime he needs to. I do ask him to use his lamp and to take breaks to protect his eyes, but I do not interrupt the process unless it is really necessary. Privacy in developing their skills sometimes means absence from my own supervision. A sense of being watched can quickly change my children's behavior. Sometimes they are embarrassed by the realization that they have been "caught" while lost in play.

Creative activities are sometimes part of our curriculum, but usually they are performed outside of the time we spend in regular subjects like Bible, language arts, math, history, and science/nature. Because all my children are currently in elementary grades, we are able to get through most of our "schoolwork" within three to five hours, which leaves plenty of time for the imagination.

Participate!

We can enliven our children's experiences simply by participating with them. We have the responsibility as parents to develop their initiative into appropriate actions. We also have the responsibility to set their spirits free! By enjoying music and the arts with them while they are young, we are granting unspoken "permission" to sing and dance or color lively pictures or build a tent with sheets and enjoy hours inside a makeshift playhouse. They desperately want to know that their playful expressions are "okay," and there is no better way to convince them of this than to join them.

Every spring I pull out my watercolors in response to the blooming flowers. I am not an accomplished painter, but I will not allow my lack of professionalism to rob me of the attempt to have fun creating beautiful paintings, especially in the privacy of my own home. I always invite Will to join me, and he always does. We spread our supplies out and I stare at the flower I have chosen, while he draws from pictures in his head. I ask him for help with shading and various other things. I always ask him if he likes my picture, just as he asks me what I think of his. In this way we enter into the artistic process together. It is one of those occasions where our age difference means very little because, for a brief moment, we are beginners together.

Sometimes our children need our guidance to enrich their experiences. I have observed Katie's countenance change dramatically when Michael sits by her side and plays piano with her. Her smile grows as large as that of the Cheshire cat, and her laughter begins to fill the room. Often, the puppet theater will stand unused until Mom prompts the children to play by putting on a show herself. After a few moments, I quietly leave the room while they begin making up their own stories in response to the beckoning puppets.

Our participation also communicates to our children that we want to spend time with them. The best way to reinforce all of our hugs, kisses, and whispered "I love you's" is to give them a portion of our time. The time we spend with our children demonstrates to them the depth of our affection. While our absence speaks louder than words, our involved presence shouts! By participating in activities that interest them, I enter into their world, and my presence alone encourages and affirms who they are and who they hope to become.

Role Models and Mentors

When we hired her, we had no idea that the new part-time baby-sitter we had employed for the summer months was an art major. We thought that we were helping a future college student raise some money, but we were pleasantly surprised at how much we were helped. There was no way to anticipate the effect this new comrade would have on Will and the other children. Hindsight reveals the beauty of God's grace on our home that summer and what has resulted from Jennifer's presence and willingness to share her gifts.

The first clue that something special was happening was the extraordinary amount of paper we were going through. The second was the strange quiet that descended over the house. In our home, quiet usually meant something had gone awry, that someone was into something he or she had no business with. But when I would set out to discover the cause of the unusual peacefulness, I would invariably find the children hovering around Jennifer, who was drawing whatever they asked of her, and drawing it well. Will did not participate much at first, but it was soon evident that through watching an artist at work his pump was being primed. By the end of the summer, his observation had brought forth its effect. There came an overflow of creative drawings from him with much more detail than ever before. This experience taught us something very important about the role a "mentor" from outside the family could play.

A year later we were present at a homeschool seminar on the arts. This particular day a cartoonist was speaking. When, following his talk, he had the children participate in different drawings, Will was truly in his element. So when we found out that the cartoonist gave private lessons, we thought it would be good to give it a try. Once again, we have been delighted with our experience and would recommend it to other parents. Art lessons, music lessons, drama, or dancing can all be taught by a talented teacher and bring much benefit to our children.

The instructor we use believes that all children have the capability within them to draw. The trick is to develop the gift that is already there. He instructs by entering into the world of his student, rather than lecturing or following a set regime. Instead he asks his young artists, "So, what are we going to draw today? What has been on your mind this week?" For Will, the answers come easy. He seems to always be thinking about something. His interests vary from helicopters to reptiles, dinosaurs, trucks, spiders, and bugs. "Monsters" was his reply one week.

He had been wondering if there were any monsters in the Bible. Michael read to him from the Book of Job, where there is a vivid description of the "leviathan." The next week, Will's instructor had him bring his Bible along, and verse by verse they wrote down the characteristics of this awesome creature. Then, side by side they worked, drawing the image that came to their minds, being careful with the details. Naturally, the resulting pictures were quite different from each other. But they served as a valuable lesson on the uniqueness of perspective.

My participation in Will's world of art is very meaningful. But I can do very little, if anything at all, to advance his skill. This is an area where people in our communities can be a valuable resource. And this interaction itself teaches important lessons. I can think of no better provision for my children, outside the home, than a human relationship that equips them to become not only better artists, but also better individuals.

Encouragement

Creativity is a personal process—a process which can sometimes cause one to feel isolated and alone. It can take the eye that recognizes beauty and turn it in a critical manner upon its owner with stinging self-criticism. We can be our own harshest judges. People in the process of creating need to hear words of encouragement. Whether it is a professional like Michael who is composing a song to go on his sixteenth album or a child who picks up crayons for the first time, we are all fragile people in need of approval. Through creativity we are expressing something from deep within ourselves. We need to be encouraged in our honest attempts, because we all need love and acceptance to grow to our full potential.

> May our Lord Jesus Christ himself and God our Father, who loved us and by his grace gave us eternal encouragement and good hope, encourage your hearts and strengthen you in every good deed and word (2 Thessalonians 2:16,17).

Michael's Perspective
The Bible and the Compulsion to Create

Last night there was a visual feast in the sky. The comet of the century, Hale-Bopp, rose early in the night, visible just after sunset. We waited out the dusk, straining to be the first to see the ghostlike sight of the comet low on the horizon. Then, all at once, there it was! In the darkening sky we could just make out the tail, pointing away from the sun (though the direction of the tail does not indicate the direction the comet is traveling). Just as we were beginning to get used to the sight, we looked over our shoulders, and there was a dazzling full moon. It was as if, jealous for the attention, it had risen in all its glory to lure us away from our single-minded focus on the comet. We knew that in a few hours there was going to be a lunar eclipse. Sure enough, later in the evening, the earth's shadow began to creep across the pockmarked face of the moon, until it was a mysterious brick-red color. Adding to the drama, the planet Mars was shining a brilliant red just below the moon. Soon two enormous meteors came streaking across the sky, both leaving sparkling trails. It was an amazing evening!

Will stayed outside for most of this celestial feast. On first seeing the comet, he gasped, "Thank You, Lord!" When I called him back out a few hours later to see the height of the eclipse, he whispered, "Praise the Lord for the moon."

My eight-year-old understands innately what many of us have forgotten: The beauty of the creation is a reminder of the beauty of God. But not everyone seems capable of seeing this truth. The next morning we heard on the news the first rumors of a cult group which had committed mass suicide. As the bizarre details unfolded, it came to light that the tragedy was somehow connected to the comet. The maniacal leader of the "Heaven's Gate" cult had spoken to his followers about an alien spacecraft which was lurking close behind the comet, preparing to evacuate the true believers from the earth and usher them into a higher plane of existence. They were instructed to commit suicide as a way to prepare themselves for meeting with the aliens. What had been such a beautiful, faith-building experience for my son and me, a reminder of God's glory and beauty, had been for these misguided souls a sign to take their own lives. It was in one sense a betrayal of the beauty of the comet, a treacherous trick of the evil one to rob the momentous celestial event of its power to speak of the Creator.

God, as we first meet Him in the pages of the Bible, is a creative Artist, working away at His creation, stepping back at the end of each day, casting a loving but critical eye at His work and concluding that it is "good." But creativity doesn't end with the act of creation in Genesis 1. A close look reveals that throughout the Bible we see the subject of creativity addressed again and again.

After the world was made, God gave a mandate—a command—to the woman and the man to "be fruitful." Along with that mandate they were told to care for creation creatively, to tend the garden God had given them. I have often wondered if the Lord placed within all things, along with the drives connected with reproducing after their kind, a compulsion to create. This is a compulsion to be creative, to produce works of beauty which mirror the beauty the first man and woman experienced in the garden of God. There is inside of each of us a drive, a compulsion to create, to be obedient to the creative mandate first given to Adam and Eve. If this is true, and I believe it is, it would explain much about mankind and why so many are driven to create in spite of themselves. My mentor, Bill Lane, says it even explains why people doodle as they talk on the phone. Gene Veith has referred to it as the "universal habit of decoration."

But the discussion of creativity in the Bible does not end with the Creation story. As we move on in Scripture, we see a vivid display of this compulsion as Noah builds an enormous boat (450 feet long, 75 feet high) for a flood that had not happened, at a time before it had ever rained! This unusual drive must have been a puzzlement not only to his neighbors, but to Noah himself as well (Genesis 6). After his sea voyage, the creative mandate which was first given to Adam and Eve is reissued to Noah (Genesis 9). Several chapters later, in Genesis 11, we see an example of creativity gone bad. The men of Babel decide to construct a tower to exalt themselves and their civilization. Here is creativity as betrayal, and the price paid is the confusion of language which brings the project to a halt.

Exodus 25–31 records the construction of the marvelous tabernacle of the Lord, in which every type of visual art is represented. It is significant to note that the first person ever described as being "filled with the Spirit" was Bezalel (Exodus 31:1ff), the artist who was to oversee the construction of the tabernacle. Many years later comes the temple of

Solomon, where again God is involved in every creative detail of the planning and construction of this breathtaking building. Later still, we see Ezra and Nehemiah driven to risk their lives in the reconstruction of both the temple and the wall of the city of Jerusalem.

In the original creative mandate issued to Adam and Eve, the call of God was to work with the creation in such a way as to cause it to bring forth further praise to the Creator. Creativity is a spontaneous, inward, oftentimes inexplicable response to the mandate issued by God to His creature king and queen. It is connected to our bearing of His image. It is, ultimately, a mystery.

This creativity often expresses itself in music. In the Writings (the poetic books of the Old Testament), we see a preoccupation with singing a "new song." The act of writing and singing the new song signifies that the truth contained in the Scriptures has in fact become a reality to the community of believers. By singing the new song, they have made it their own. By announcing at the opening of the psalm that it is in fact "new," the psalmist is reaffirming that, like the mercies of the Lord, so too the creative gift, with its ability to express the deep things of God, is indeed "new." It is a fresh outpouring and, like the manna, is never meant to be hoarded, but to be collected in the right amount to feed God's people.

As a songwriter, I can tell you that the greatest moment of encouragement comes not from awards or high chart numbers, but from the sharing of a "new" song for the first time. To sing new words and notes for the very first time, to wonder as you're doing it whether they will have the desired effect on the listener (be it the people or God), is the joy of the Christian musician. The sharing of the new song is an experience unlike any other.

The Bible expresses this as well:

Psalm 33:3—"Sing to him a new song; play skillfully, and shout for joy."

Psalm 40:3—"He put a new song in my mouth, a hymn of praise to our God."

Psalm 96:1—"Sing to the LORD a new song; sing to the LORD, all the earth."

Psalm 98:1—"Sing to the LORD a new song, for he has done marvelous things."

Psalm 144:9—"I will sing a new song to you, O God; on the ten-stringed lyre I will make music to you."

Psalm 149:1—"Sing to the LORD a new song, his praise in the assembly of the saints."

(See also Revelation 5:9— "And they sang a new song: 'You are worthy to take the scroll and to open its seals . . .'" and Revelation 14:3—"And they sang a new song before the throne and before the four living creatures and the elders.")

As we move on to the prophetical books, we are introduced to yet another category in the realm of creativity: the concept of "burden." In fact, the Hebrew word for *prophecy* literally means "burden." How do the prophets respond to this sense of bearing a burden? They sing! Prophecy is almost always poetry. "Bring in the musicians that I may prophecy!" We see this even in the renewal of prophecy in the Gospel of Luke at the advent of Jesus. Mary, Elizabeth, Simeon, and Anna all broke forth in prophecy in response to their new sense of a God-given burden, and so new songs in praise of the Lord were brought forth.

Isaiah is filled with poetic images. He speaks of the sun and moon being ashamed, of the trees clapping their hands, of God as a Rock. Throughout the writings of the prophets, we see God's great attempt to recapture the imaginations of His people by the use of vision, metaphor, and parable, as well as the sometimes bizarre actions of the prophets, which come in response to their deep sense of burden.

Being the Creator-Artist that He is, the great Romancer, the perfectly loving Father, God calls out to us through the prophets. He sings to us, paints images in our minds through the visions of the prophets. These sounds and songs, these visions and images, stand at the door of our own imaginations and knock. Through them God opens the door of His own inner life to us. He paints pictures of His hopes for our future, as well as His worst nightmares of what is waiting for us if we choose to go on living without Him. He pleads for us to open the eyes of our hearts, to hear with our ears, to really understand. This is the heart of prophecy: God speaking to us in such a way as to recapture our imaginations. The prophets teach us to learn from, to hunger for, to listen to God's voice. They acquaint us with the "how" of how He speaks. Through them we learn to listen to the whole of God's Word in new ways. From the example of the prophets we discover that God is speaking through the parables of our daily lives, in the silence of prayer, in the good news of creation. They open our eyes to a vision as grand as the greatest of their own visions, to a world alive with God speaking at every turn in our lives, in every moment, no matter how mundane it may seem. Through the prophets we begin to glimpse a God who loves us so much He wants to be married to us, who longs to embrace us as Father, who ultimately comes to us as Son.

At last, with the incarnation, we see the creativity of God literally come to life! The focus of the New Testament is Jesus, who, though He never paints a picture or writes a song (we hear Him sing only once), leads the most richly creative life ever lived. His life, the things He said and did, have continued capturing the imaginations of men and women for 2000 years. His life is beautifully simple, yet deeply profound (the essence of profundity is simplicity). His dealing with others demonstrates remarkable creativity (e.g., the discourse with Nicodemus or the dialogue with the Sadducees over the woman married seven times). He encourages the incorrigibles, and makes outcasts, prostitutes, and tax collectors all feel God's acceptance. In Christ we see a Person who refuses to compartmentalize His life. His creative imagination pervades every aspect of His life. He is creativity come alive! In fact, an important part of the early church's confession of who Jesus is included the affirmation that it was through Him that the creation happened (John 1, Colossians 1, Hebrews 1).

Where does all this biblical emphasis on creativity lead us? How are we to teach our children to respond to the creative mandate of God? First, we must realize that creativity is a part of the image of God in them. That is, all of us are called to creativity, to be creative as an act of obedience. If this is true, then a central part of our role as homeschooling parents is to help our children identify their individual creative giftings. Perhaps they may be creative musicians, perhaps (as important) they may be creative listeners to the music of others. Maybe their specific gifting is in the visual arts, the written word, or in their interactions with others. We must expand our own understanding of creativity in light of the life of Jesus, and assist our children in maturing in their individual gift.

Finally, and perhaps most fundamentally, we need to teach our children that their creativity is a part of bearing the image of God. We must lead them to a fresh awareness of the call of the creative mandate on their lives. We must encourage them to create "new" works, to become infected with the biblical preoccupation for singing the new song.

FIVE

Stepping in Time to the Music

So look in the mirror and
pray for the grace
To tear off the mask, see the
art of your face
Open your earlids to hear the sweet song
Of each moment that passes
and pray to prolong

Lyric from "The Poem of Your Life" / *Poiema*
Words and Music by Michael Card
Used by permission

*O*ne might assume that because Michael is a writer, lyricist, and musician by trade, music would be the constant focus in our home, and that we would be aggressive in exposing our children to good music in an attempt to develop them into budding musicians. Not so. Music in our home has no greater precedence than any other form of "education through exposure." Reading great literature, gazing at the stars, learning responsibility through chores, praying for our community at home and abroad, browsing through resource books—all these things are important to a well-rounded education. Music is just one of these elements. But it is an important element. In his own ministry, Michael has found that music is one of the most effective tools to communicate the gospel beautifully and effectively.

While it may not have precedence over other subjects in the context of education, music is part of the weft in the tapestry of our lives. It is one of the background colors that other colors play upon. Music is our livelihood and part of the context of our family life. It serves as such a powerful tool of communication that we respect it for its worth.

Music Is a Gift

First and foremost, music is a gift from the Lord. From the heights of the heavens to the depths of the oceans, there is some form of music to be heard. It is for us humans the most common form of praise and worship. When we encounter beauty or truth, or when we as individuals encounter the love of the Lord in some form or another, our reaction is often the desire to sing. Really, how can any of us restrain ourselves when encountering our Creator? Michael has acknowledged for years that his songs come from an overflow of his walk with the Lord.

It is important to realize that the Lord has given music to everyone, not just to those who have been gifted. Because we live in a culture that lifts up the successful professional musician, we need to emphasize to our children that music is for everyone. They need to know that they should not discredit themselves just because they are not naturally gifted as a singer or musician. We need to encourage their desire to explore this mysterious gift that is waiting to be opened.

The Role of Music

Music enhances our lives. All of us, whether we simply join fervently in singing the hymns and choruses at church on Sunday or are under the glare of the spotlight on the concert stage, can find the richness that music brings to our lives. It is a gift for us all, one that brings with it the heights and depths of emotion.

I will never forget the confusion on Will's young face the first time he cried because of joy. We had just finished watching a touching movie together, one that had a particularly poignant ending. As a broken relationship was mended in the film, the music swelled into a joyful chorus. Will said amidst his sobs, "Mommy, I don't understand why I'm crying and the music is so happy. I just can't help it."

Somehow, chord progressions and rhythm have a way of making us feel joy to the point of tears, or exhilaration that makes us want to cry out with our longings. This mysterious thing called music allows us to engage with life at a depth and breadth that God wants us to experience. It enhances our lives in a number of ways.

Music enhances our lives through relaxation. In a very utilitarian use, it lulls babies to sleep. We had the incredible convenience of Michael writing two lullaby albums at the time our children were infants. *Sleep Sound in Jesus* and *Come to the Cradle* have been played numerous times in our nurseries over the last few years. Although we had personally experienced its calming effects, the power of music to relax us came to me powerfully when Michael and I were in Atlanta for the National Youth Specialties Conference. After Michael's presentation, I was greeted by several couples. They were all sharing stories with me of how *Sleep Sound in Jesus* had ministered to their families.

One couple in particular told me that their infant was born three months premature and the doctors did not give their little girl much hope. At this stage of prematurity, infants frequently die of cardiac arrest because their little hearts beat so fast and furiously that they collapse under the strain. This couple had taken a tape recorder to the hospital and played the lullabies for their daughter. As she lay there, hooked up to several machines, the gentle sounds came forth from the tape recorder. The mother realized that something unusual was happening. As the music would play, she could actually see the heart rate slowing down on the heart monitor. "My baby is now three years old, and I just wanted you to know the impact that your husband's music had on our family," she said to me.

This, of course, is a very dramatic illustration of the relaxing qualities of music. But all of us have experienced the peacefulness that good music can bring to our lives. Many of us experience relaxation when we turn on our car stereo or listen to classical music during a meal. In the Old Testament,

David was called in many times to soothe Saul's anxiety by playing music in his presence. In music, the Lord has given us a wonderful way to relax in the midst of our often harried lives. For that we are most grateful.

Music also enhances our lives by bringing families and friends together to listen to and play music. Through all the traveling we did while I was growing up, our beloved piano was the one piece of furniture that followed us everywhere. It was during our stay in England that it really came to life for me. I would prepare for school as my older brother and sister would practice for their piano lessons. The joyful sounds of Beethoven's "Fur Elise," or one of Mozart's many concertos would dance in my head as I walked to school, humming the infectious melodies. The enthusiasm my siblings felt for music served to whet my own appetite for the time when I would be old enough to take lessons as well. Somehow the music they produced, even though it was imperfectly performed, caused me to gravitate toward the room they were practicing in, to watch and listen, looking forward to the melodies that had become my favorites.

Years later I could be found sitting at my brother's feet while he played guitar or banjo. These were the only times during the tumultuous teenage years that we really got along. His vulnerability to share his gifts softened my critical tongue, and I learned to compliment him and enjoy his company. Music taught me to let down my guard, to be vulnerable as a listener in response to the vulnerability of the performer. After my father retired from the Air Force, we took my brother's lead and gathered many nights on the farm with guitars and banjos. A supportive laughter at those of us brave enough to attempt playing a new instrument would fill our living room. Silence would then follow as we delighted in the talent of the one who dared to share.

Music enhances our lives by giving us a depth of emotion, a sense of relaxation, and by bringing us together through plain fun and sharing. It is a gift of expression for those daring enough to use it to express themselves. When I think of the way music is woven into our life at home, a tapestry comes to mind, woven of only a few prominent colors. In the tapestry of our lives, the color that is music has a special place. But it is not music alone. All the different aspects of our lives intermingle, and it is the combination of the colors that makes the beauty of the weave.

Making Music

Too often when we think of music we think of the performance side: of piano lessons and recitals, of encouraging our children to learn to play an instrument, of badgering them to practice. Sadly, we sometimes can forget to teach them how to appreciate music through "listening." Learning to play notes and to interpret melody is most certainly a worthwhile endeavor. But learning to enjoy music through listening is every bit as important and can be the vessel to transport our souls beyond the limitations of our own ability.

We have taught the children how to listen to different instruments by making it a game. On most of Michael's albums there is an orchestral piece without lyrics. When Will and Katie were younger, we were listening to the orchestral piece on *Present Reality*. They responded by making up stories to go with the music, as they had learned to do with "Peter and the Wolf," a delightful piece we had already exposed them to. Without fully understanding all the technicalities of music, they were responding to the chord progressions, the rhythm, the transitions from gaiety to intensity. Soon they had learned to identify different instruments as having their own unique characteristics. As Will would say, "There goes that violin again, trying to make me cry."

By simply providing a good variety of tapes or CDs, we build on their innate ability to respond to what they hear. Our responsibility is to make sure they have good music to listen to. We have found it worthwhile to read about the great composers and listen to their music. Not only does it hone their listening skills, teaching them to become discerning in their tastes, but it also provides valuable exposure to the people and places of that composer's particular time period in history.

Music is God's gift to us. Our lives are richer and stronger for having it, as it provides an immeasurable source of expression. Our joy is made all the more joyful and our sorrow all the more real to us by the power of music. Michael and I both experience immense benefit from expressing ourselves through music. Music is the overflow of the depth of Michael's personal walk with the Lord. Compared to him, my musical abilities are rather amateur, but I find few things more delightful than sitting at the piano and playing my favorite hymns.

Because Michael makes his living through music, we have come across subtle expectations to deliver another performer. But it is characteristic of his own attitudes that Michael does not encourage anyone, especially his own children, to become "success-driven" performers. Rather, he encourages musicians to serve their communities and applies the same suggestion to his own child. Katie did not start piano lessons until she was nine years old. She did not have the maturity or the motivation to deal with the responsibility of practicing for her lessons. The decision to wait has proven to be a good one. She plays the piano every day in response to her need and desire to express herself. I seldom have to remind her to practice. After we read our morning devotions, we huddle around the piano and Katie picks out the hymn to sing. She does not play perfectly, but that is not the point. In our home environment, we enjoy the process every bit as much as the performance.

> The LORD is my strength and my shield; my heart trusts in him, and I am helped. My heart leaps for joy and I will give thanks to him in song (Psalm 28:7).

Walking with Dad

Having a father who makes his living from writing and singing does make our life unique in certain ways. But in most ways we are a normal family. This very morning, Michael and I were up at 4 A.M. I was to benefit from two hours of solitude to write, while Michael was off fly-fishing with his best friend and the children were still asleep. He has promised me trout when he returns! In the meantime, the children and I will face our day as any other: sorting through new information and saving questions for Dad to answer over a fish dinner.

The first question the children will ask this morning is, "Mom, where's Dad?" This is the question they ask every morning unless he is already up making coffee or a fake cappuccino for Will. Often the answer is that he is still sleeping because he was up late working. This is one of the unique qualities of walking the journey with a father who is an artist. Artists and writers require large blocks of un-interrupted time for practicing their craft. Often the most available uninterrupted hours are those which stretch far into the wee morning hours.

This morning was unusual. Rarely does Dad leave the house just for fun. His playful jaunt was a spontaneous decision squeezed into an otherwise overcrowded and de-manding schedule. Within the year are months set aside for Michael to do research, to study, and to write. He is home during this season working in a small one-room Shaker building that sits only a few yards from the house. We are disciplined as a family to respect his solitude while work-ing, but he has made it perfectly clear that even though his door is closed, he will quickly open it if we are in need of him. Occasionally, Katie visits him to play his electric key-board just to be near him. Will may get a chance to play on his computer during one of his visits. The point is, they have opportunity to explore Dad's work area and be with him in short intervals while he writes. When I answer their question in the morning with, "Dad is already working this morning," they know where he is, they know how to pray for him, and they know what is required of them for him to complete his task.

Michael's schedule during the writing season is not simple. On top of research and writing, there are business meetings to attend in preparation for the future tour or maintenance of office needs. There are interviews and speaking engagements and a constant stream of unanswered letters waiting for the response that he always gives.

Our schedule in schooling is what remains somewhat constant. It has to be if we are to meet the state requirements and attain our personal goal of excellence through education. The advantage of Michael being home is that he always checks in. I sometimes need to hear his approval on a "job well done." He clearly communicates that what we are doing is important by joining in with us when he can. This is something that all fathers should try to make a priority. We are never too busy to give time to our family!

What is important in their daily interaction with Michael is the fact that the children really care about what their father is doing. This is because he cares about what they are doing! Michael takes their walks and talks seriously. He has nurtured a relationship with them that goes beyond parent/child, stretching into mentor/student and, dare I say it, friends? Charlotte Mason, who believed that it was always a mistake to "talk down" to children, would be pleased by the lack of "twaddle" that goes on in our home. The children are talked to as they are—young people whose opinions and ideas we respect.

On the Road . . . Again!

The season for concert touring is the hardest part of the year. This is when we feel the sacrifice of what Michael is called to do. The dull ache that all of us feel in his absence is associated with the very thing that comforts us. It is music that calls the children's father away, but it is also music that allows our family to stay in touch with him. Even though he leaves us with plenty of letters and cards to pore over in his absence, noth-ing can replace the sound of his voice. We have the advantage of hearing it anytime we want by putting one of his discs in the player. Somehow, through the songs on his tapes and CDs, we are comforted and are lead to the Comforter through the truth revealed in the lyrics.

The advantage of touring is that we occasionally get to join him. Usually it is for short weekends, but we try to make the most of them. We make it special by finding a museum, a zoo, or some other point of interest. Katie went alone with Michael to Birmingham, Alabama, and visited and revisited the chapel at Samford University. The murals captivated her, and she shared each scene with her dad in great detail. Sights that are easily available are sometimes overlooked.

We have been surprised by how little effort it takes to provide a great educational experience. Next time you are planning a vacation, you might consider the educational
opportunities that are available in the area of the country
you are visiting. That is one of the great advantages of homeschooling: the classroom always travels with you!

The primary purpose of traveling with Dad, however,
is to become aware of what is required of him when he is
on the road. Michael shares his prayer requests with the
children, as well as his concerns about the performance, or
his weariness from travel. He engages them to join with
him in the responsibility of prayer. When we travel with
him, he lets the children know how happy he is that they
could be along with comments like, "I'm so glad you're
here with me!" His hugs and words of encouragement let
them know that they are always welcome in his life, even
while he is working.

Tools of the Trade

One of the interesting things about what Michael does
is the variety of instruments used in recording the songs.
He is always looking out for new and interesting musical
instruments. We have a set of African drums made out of
bones that he purchased at a missionary shop. We have an
Irish drum called a bodhran. Recently, he brought home a
harmonium. As we study geography, these wonderful instruments take us to the countries they come from, giving
us a window into another culture and introducing us to
new sounds.

The varieties of music are an important tool for Michael
in his songwriting. During Michael's work on his last
album, we listened to African music, and the album before
that we listened to Gregorian chants. Our favorite type of
music, and one Michael has used extensively in his newer
compositions, is Irish. This has become our family's unani-
mous favorite!

On occasion, the children are able to go to the studio during a recording. This has been an amazing experience for teaching them to appreciate the greatest instrument of all: the human voice. It is a thrilling process to watch someone sing and to hear the voice of what you think might be an angel. Katie and I were speechless while Christine Dente sang her parts for *Come to the Cradle*. Steve Green has gifted us with his participation in musical projects, and once again we sat in awe. Recently, on *Unveiled Hope*, Michael's album on the Book of Revelation, we sat at the feet of our favorite black gospel choir, Covenant Ensemble. The variety is testimony to God's wonderful creation.

Learning to Listen

As I have already emphasized, one does not have to be in the music business to appreciate music. The quality of recordings and our modern equipment to play them on is so well perfected that anyone can have the sense of being in the studio. The key to music appreciation is learning the art of "listening."

I grew up listening to music: a variety of records, tapes, the radio, and live entertainment from my own home. At least, I thought I was listening. But it was Michael who really taught me how to truly listen. When we were still in college, we would listen to Dan Fogelberg, James Taylor, or Michael McDonald. Michael would point out how the instruments were being used and the artful complexity of the arrangements. I had not been in the habit of listening this carefully, of breaking down the arrangements in an attempt to hear each specific instrument and the part it plays. But once I glimpsed how much more meaningful this made my listening, it was like throwing open a new door of appreciation. To this day, when he has completed an album, we all sit down and listen to every detail.

Listening to music requires your full attention in the same way that reading a book does. It deserves the kind of concentration that is necessary to write a letter. When you use music simply as background noise, as so many people seem to do, you miss the wonderful detail of expression that comes from the arrangers and producers.

One of my favorite arrangements was one done for Michael by Alan Moore. He wrote a song titled "Traitor's Look," based on the narrative about Judas's betrayal from Luke 22:3-6. The lyric makes reference to the sea of doubt that the betrayer seems to fall into:

> How heavy was the money bag
> That couldn't set you free
> It became a heavy millstone
> As you fell into the sea.

The strings rise and fall as ocean waves throughout the song—a musical touch that most will miss if they are not listening carefully. Of course, the studio musicians have a great deal to do with the success of the arrangement. And the better they are, the more freedom they are given to interpret the melody. Producers and arrangers count on these men and women a great deal. They are, sadly, taken for granted as songs come and go, and as we mass-produce ever more music.

By giving time and attention to the finer points of music, we show our children a quiet respect for the lives behind the songs, teaching them to imagine what it must be like to write and perform music.

Music in the Home

As with any other resource you plan to provide for your children, ready availability of a variety of music is very important. Access to tapes and CDs at the appropriate age gives your children freedom to explore music, much like a library of books gives them freedom to browse. We have a variety of tapes and CDs available for their listening enjoyment. As with any other form of artistry that engages our imagination, we guard what we listen to, excluding musical "twaddle"! In this context, I mean music that is "played down" to children—silly and artless work that shows no respect for their intelligence. Michael's music has been labeled as deep, as heavily theological, only for serious listeners. But our children, and the children of most of our friends, have no trouble at all understanding the biblical ideas that Michael weaves into his songs. When they have questions, they simply ask. But the insights from his songs have proved to be a great help in deepening their understanding of biblical events. For this reason, I have included in the appendix a guide that shows which biblical texts are illustrated by which songs. I hope you find it as helpful a tool as I have.

Up to this point, I have mostly emphasized inspirational music. But this is not the only kind of music we want to make a place for in our home. We have also started a musical library of classical music and of various different kinds of music that Michael has used in research.

We enjoy listening to the beauty of the work of the great classical composers. There is a richness here I would like to be part of my children's world. When we listen, I like to correlate the great composers with the historical time periods we are studying. As often as I can, I try to integrate their lives and works with our history lessons. When we were reading about the American War of Independence in 1775, for example, we discovered that Ludwig van Beethoven was a five-year-old living in Germany. To learn about the composers, we have found several valuable resources. *The Milton Cross New Encyclopedia of the Great Composers and Their Music* is an in-depth reference work that is full of good information. More fun for the children is the entertaining "Classical Kids" series, a tape series combining the composer's music with a dramatic story. We are currently working to build a library of great classical music. There is so much available that it can be kind of confusing trying to decide what to buy. I have found the list of great classical works listed in Terry Glaspey's book *Children of a Greater God* to be an invaluable help in finding some of the best and most accessible pieces of classical music. It helps me as I work through the lives of the composers and build our musical library.

The exploration of music in our home is primarily a source of joy. Like joy, it is most often spontaneous and impulsive. It is one of the rare subjects that can yield great benefits without exhaustive academic preparation. Because it can be such a great vehicle for beauty, it can also be a window through which we can experience the beauty of God.

Michael's Perspective
The Power of Music

Socrates once said that "when the soul hears music, it drops its best guard." That, for me, is one of the best descriptions of the power that music has. With music it is possible to open a door in the heart of the listener. Once inside, the musician can either beautify the interior of that soul or desecrate that most holy of places. Often if you can get someone to sing something, you can get them to believe it. This has been used for good as well as evil throughout history. Music is a truly powerful tool.

Today I asked my son Will what he was feeling as he listened to a piece of music. "It feels like I'm flying on wings," he said with his eyes clamped shut. His description points to another power music has: the power to transport us. Once again, this power can be used for good or for evil. How many times in the midst of worry or grief has a song lifted you out of that dark place and taken you to a better place, a place with more light and air? Conversely, how many times have you witnessed the grimaced faces of young (and sometimes not-so-young) people as they listened to the often torturous music variously described as heavy metal or death rock? These poor people seem not to be in their own skins as they experience the cacophonies of modern music. And indeed, many have chosen suicide on the advice of the lyrics of this dark music, or simply perhaps as a way of ending the despair and pain in their souls which the music so gruesomely magnifies.

Often while I'm on the road, parents ask me about the effects of rock music on their children. Usually they themselves are a product of the generation we might call the "era of rock," so I sometimes get the feeling that they are asking as much for themselves as for their children. After giving the matter a lot of thought over the years, I have concluded that the greatest long-term danger of rock/metal music is not the worldly value system it represents, or even the often dark associations that affect its listener. The worst lasting effect it has is that it teaches kids not to listen at all. It conditions them to tune out the words in favor of the overpowering music. That can have a devastating effect on the soul. Music can, for all its good potential, rob us of the ability to listen to the word.

Music also has the power of shaping our lives and value systems. It can be so powerful and consuming a force that we can give our lives to it. This is something I've seen all too many times in my experience as a musician. I have known those whose language, dress, style of living, and values were all dictated by a style of music. Once while I was paying for some gasoline, the teller asked, "You're a musician, aren't you?"

To which I replied in horror, "How did you know?"

"You just looked like one," he said with a smile, not knowing he had just ruined my whole day!

So what are we to do with this power, this dynamite that can be used both to destroy lives as well as to blast away stubborn mountains that may stand in our way? Once again, as with any important question, we turn to the life of Jesus for the answer. The Word tells us that everything must be brought under submission to Christ, and this especially applies to the power of music.

But what does it mean to say that we are to bring the

power of music into submission to Christ? Essentially it means that we are determining to make music, like every other area of our lives, subservient to Him. It means that we will not allow this area of our lives to detract or in any other way take away from the purpose of the gospel. At the same time, we are also committing to the notion that music can be—indeed *must* be—made to serve Christ, His kingdom, and His people.

This translates into our homeschooling experience as we seek to use music to enrich the lives of our children. We teach them that the beauty of music can speak of the beauty of God. We also teach them that they must be aware of the power music holds over human hearts and emotions. But at the same time, our children can learn that they need not fear this power, as long as it is kept in its proper place.

Finally, the greatest power inherent in music is its ability to facilitate worship. Again, this power is often mishandled, even sometimes by Christians, and used to focus worshipful attention toward the musician and away from Christ. This, we must maintain, is a betrayal of the darkest and most severe kind—a betrayal of the beauty of God, an act of idolatry.

Therefore, we must pass on to our children a biblical value system which is shaped by an awareness of the power and true purpose of music. We must listen along with them to the music of their generation and help them make responsible choices in terms of what they will listen to and why. Above all, we must by the witness of our own lives demonstrate to them how music can be used to serve Christ and worship Him in Spirit and truth.

A Steep Path
to Climb

Dealing with Learning Difficulties

So soak up like a sponge
All that's joyful and best
And squeeze yourself out
Upon those who are blessed
A God given gift
Is wrapped up in you
You show more of Him
Than I'll ever teach you

Lyric from "Nathan's Song" / *Come to the Cradle*
Words and Music by Michael Card
Used by permission

From Michael's journal for Nathan—October 26, 1992:

*Y*ou were born at 10:51 this morning. I was the first one to see your face, even before your mom. You were perfect.

You were taken over to a warm table to be washed while your mom recovered. The nurse wrapped you up, put a little stocking cap on your head, and handed you to me. It was a moment I will never forget.

Your grandmothers were waiting outside. They were overjoyed to see you too. Later everyone was in the room talking and carrying on. I just wanted to hold you and spend time with you. Later on I got a chance to do just that.

My love hasn't been divided a third time, but rather multiplied by three. You will never understand this until you're a father.

Anyway, on this day you came out into the world, to be with us for a little while. We're glad you're here and that, for a time, you are ours.

I love you,
Your Dad

Michael and I have kept journals for all the children from the day they were born. We write in them from time to time in an effort to record traces of the steps they have taken. We also write in response to our appreciation for their lives. This was the first entry in Nathan's journal. We did not know at the time just how precious he would become to us.

There was no indication when we brought Nathan home from the hospital that there was anything unusual about him. He was a beautiful baby boy responding to his first few days of life like any other. He was three months old before I was suspicious of something being different.

I am still not certain what it was that made me wonder if Nathan reacted to the mobile over his crib differently than his siblings. He seemed to stare at it endlessly. It took more effort to distract him from it than it would have for my other children. Was it, I asked myself, just my protective nature as a mother feeding negative thoughts into my imagination, or was my observation accurate? A few months later I noticed his attention being drawn to the movement of ceiling fans. He would focus on them so intently that he did not always respond to the other things happening around him. I also found that I had to work harder at engaging him than the other children. Once again, I was not quite sure of myself. Was it just my imagination?

When he was two-and-a-half years old, his fascination with his brother's train began. We were thrilled that he had an interest at so young an age. We provided books on trains and began collecting Brio train tracks and Thomas the Tank Engine train cars. We were thrilled when Brio came out with a battery-operated locomotive. So was Nathan. When I observed his play, I noticed he would always lie down next to the track, following the motion of the train with his eyes. His focus was centered on the wheels turning round and round. I spent much time just observing his play to see what I could learn. He would play so contentedly by himself that it actually seemed that he preferred to play alone.

He was not speaking much at all by age three. And during this time in his life he was more easily agitated during the course of the day. As he approached an age level that required him to interact more with the world around him, we noticed that he was frequently angry and would scream and cry in frustration. A feeling of emotional chaos began to dawn over the household, and little by little Michael and I began feeling a sense of defeat. We were not getting through to Nathan and could do little to comfort him when he was upset. The temper tantrums were unpredictable. There was no rhyme or reason to them, at least that I could discern. Now that we are further along the path, I know what upsets him. I understand his perspective more clearly, and know there is usually a valid reason for his outbursts. But at that time I was completely perplexed by his actions.

There were times Nathan would become aggressive toward the other children or toward me, hitting and kicking or throwing objects across the room. His language was not developed well enough to communicate his grievances, which only seemed to fuel the flame of his inward turmoil. I noticed that in times of great stress he would take on a daydreaming type of expression, looking off into the distance and not focusing on anything in particular. Or, more frightening, he would find a place to sit or lie down and repose in a listless position. If we picked him up during this time, he would not respond; instead, his legs and arms would hang down, not lending any support to being held. These moments were very difficult times for me emotionally. Not being able to reach my child was breaking my heart.

While life was growing more difficult for him, he had another side that offered encouragement and joy, for he was affectionate and loved to cuddle. He responded to hugs and kisses with laughter. He loved being the focus of my gentle teasing. For his age, the indications of a learning disability (which I will call a learning difficulty) were subtle and intermittent. A friend would call to check in and would ask the basic question, "How are you doing?" My response was frequently, "I am doing fine. It's just that when things are great, they are really great! But when they are bad, they are really, really bad. The intensity during hard situations is becoming too much for me sometimes." It was becoming increasingly apparent that the intensity was becoming too much for everyone. The older children were being accused of causing Nathan to scream whether they were guilty or not. And our responses were becoming less just and gentle, less patient and tranquil. We were frequently on edge. "What did you do to him?" was commonly uttered. Katie and Will were becoming as frustrated as Michael and I.

In our days of desperation, we did two things. We began praying earnestly for Nathan, certain by this time that something was wrong. Will often took initiative to pray for his baby brother, asking the Lord to "heal his mind and help him to talk soon." Once we openly acknowledged a problem and began to pray about it, we all became more patient and gentle. The second thing we did was to discuss it with our pediatrician. He suggested that we have Nathan tested. We were familiar with this route, for we had taken this step once before.

Katie's Story

Katie also had learning difficulties that had required intervention. Again, she was a beautiful, healthy baby girl showing no overt signs of any problems. She was four years old before my intuition told me that we should seek help. Her particular symptoms were very subtle and were not apparent to us until she was required to engage with the world around her by using higher language skills.

We had Katie involved in a Mother's Day Out program (MDO) when she was one year old until she was five. She attended the program twice a week during the public school year and was off during the summers. She responded very well to this structured educational playtime and looked forward to going. As she grew older, several people in our community, including the teachers in the MDO program, noticed something was amiss.

I would find myself interpreting for her when an adult would speak to her. I was just trying to make things clear. There was no source of information to indicate that she was too old to require my intervention. Intuition was the voice that made me feel that something in her communication skills was not quite right.

In between classes at church one Sunday, a friend stopped me for a brief moment in the hall. She looked down at Katie and said, "Hello, Katie!" Katie did not respond. I encouraged her to speak. "Katie, can you say hello?" She appeared to have been oblivious to the fact that she had been spoken to.

Then my friend said, "How are you doing?" Katie stared blankly. It was obvious she did not understand the question and was at a loss for words in order to answer. What she finally came out with was, "My grandmother came to my house last month."

This answer represented a typical response, for she frequently answered friendly social greetings or questions with facts that were irrelevant to the present situation. After Katie had entered her Sunday school class, I mentioned my concern about this to one of my friends. "Your daughter does not answer questions the way Katie does, and they are the same age. I don't think she understands what is being spoken to her." In an attempt to reassure me, my friend encouraged me to not compare our children. But I walked away from the encounter certain that something was not right.

At school she was not getting involved in art activities. I realized later that her lack of fine motor skills inhibited her ability to accomplish the tasks. More than once the teacher reported that she would pull her chair away from the table and face the wall. At home, she grew more agitated with friends and family members. She would bury her face in my dress or glare hatefully when they spoke to her. Both of her grandmothers asked me at different times if her hearing was okay. Now I realize that she did not know how to process what to her were meaningless words.

By responding to her peers inappropriately in her MDO class, Katie caused the children to begin to avoid her. Sometimes they would make faces when she made an inappropriate comment—one that had nothing to do with the conversations the children were having with her. Because a large percentage of communication is nonverbal, those funny looks that seemed relatively harmless were speaking rejection to her. She was developing an angry disposition that no amount of tender, loving care could draw out of her. My observation was that she was shutting down emotionally. The spark in her eyes was dissipating. I could not bear to see her light go out.

At the time, Michael was not as alarmed as I was. But he was always supportive of my desire to pursue help and direction. I went, with intangible suspicions, to our pediatrician. He showed complete respect for my opinions. He did not belittle me or make me feel as though my concerns were not worth his attention. This validation from him that I was not "crazy" in my wariness was very important to me in continuing with the process of seeking help. He asked Katie a few questions and then asked her to draw a smiling face, a stick figure, and a circle. At age four and a half, she could not coordinate her pencil to accomplish any of these tasks. He encouraged us to have her tested by a local speech and language center.

Testing

Speech, language, and hearing centers can be a valuable resource to our communities. They provide highly educated, qualified individuals who perform various diagnostic tests and screenings that measure child development in the area of hearing and communication skills. Consistent with God's way, there is order in learning. From infancy on, language develops in a specific order and goes through certain stages. Researchers have found that these stages are the same for all people around the world. Every infant from every tongue and tribe develops language in the same sequence.

Some children, for one reason or another, have difficulties developing properly from one stage to the next. Researchers are not quite sure why this happens. These children may adapt and recover to a degree, but it is preferable for them if they can be walked through the proper order of developmental stages. As one therapist explained to me, "Language requires building blocks, and if the blocks are not there to build with, you have a real problem. At some point these tools for language have to be provided."

I found the testing process a little frightening. I did not know what to expect. However, I was comforted and reassured once I got there. In our situations, we had to fill out information sheets before we arrived, telling what our concerns were. We then brought the child in for observation. Most of the screening we went through was done while I sat on the floor and played with my children. During the observation, they listened for speech patterns, vocabulary usage, and how my children interacted with me. They continued to let the children play while they conducted an interview with me. A hearing test was also given to determine if there were any physical obstacles to overcome.

I must say that I was actually relieved when Katie's test showed a problem. She was normal in every area of the test except one. There the testers discerned a significant deficit. I no longer felt like I had failed her somehow, or was letting my imagination run away with me. There was something wrong after all. My intuition had been right. There was a moment of relief before we started with the plan presented to us for her to get help.

When Nathan went through the testing process, I found it to be much more sobering. I was holding a 39-month-old child in my lap who was at the developmental age of 22 months. In infants and toddlers, a 17-month gap is a huge difference. This time the news stung. I felt heavily burdened as I climbed in the car, and I cried all the way home from sadness and worry for Nathan. I knew how steep the climb could be. Michael was reassuring. It was okay to cry, he said, but he also encouraged me to be grateful. It might have been something far worse. At the time, I could not think of anything worse. My little boy was lost in the world of his thoughts. What if he was not thinking at all?

A Helping Hand

Once our children were screened, the clinicians briefly told me what they observed. They sent us a letter that detailed everything, including the type of tests performed, the scores, and a written description of what they had observed.

With both of our children it was recommended that there should be intervention as soon as possible. We put our names on a waiting list, hoping to get an appointment time with one of their teachers. Katie was placed in a preschool class that she attended once a week. We saw results almost immediately. The class was structured to target the weak areas of communication, building vocabulary, and developing conversation skills. All the children in Katie's class were struggling with the same symptoms, so she was accepted for who she was. The smile began to return to her face. By observing the teacher's techniques, we were also given communication methods to use specifically with Katie that helped her understand us better. We were overjoyed because we felt as though someone had given our child to us a second time.

At the end of the preschool class, the teacher asked where Katie would be attending kindergarten. When I told her we planned to teach at home, she was very supportive. Because Katie's learning difficulties lie in the area of auditory processing, children like her can quickly get lost when given instruction in the context of a large classroom. They simply may not understand what is being said. They are susceptible to becoming labeled by the teacher as a troublemaker because they are easily distracted, unable to process all that is going on around them. Focusing on the task at hand in order to complete their work is a big challenge.

We homeschooled Katie through kindergarten using a literature-based program by Calvert. It involved a lot of reading. I deviated from the curriculum to adapt to Katie's special needs, but the one thing I was relentless with was reading. We read every day. I found books to captivate her and delight her. The following year I was beginning to pick up on problematic speech patterns. Charlotte Mason's concept of narration, where you have the child orally narrate back a story he or she has just heard or read, was especially valuable to me as we continued our studies. Because of the way we structured our schooling, I was able to pick up on difficulties Katie was having in processing the information. Had Katie been in a normal schooling situation, she would not have had her education so perfectly suited to her individual needs.

Further testing indicated that we needed to make further adjustments, and so we began taking her once a week for an hour-long private session. As progress was made, we attended every other week, until finally we stopped going altogether. I remain in touch with the speech center and have Katie tested every year to make sure we are on track. The staff has been so supportive of our homeschooling endeavor that I even asked Katie's last teacher to look over the curriculum I had chosen to make sure we were on target. She was very encouraging. Early intervention in Katie's situation has put us in a position to enjoy future freedoms.

At present, Nathan is in a special class with three children twice a week and is growing by leaps and bounds. The entire house is more stable because of our ability to communicate better. In Nathan's situation we have had to take one additional step in the area of behavior management.

Nathan did not understand being told no. He did not understand a pop on the leg for disobedience. In his mind, if I told him to do something, then he should be able to tell me to do something. The concept of authority was beyond his grasp. It is very difficult disciplining a child who does not understand or respect authority. Temper tantrums were occurring daily. It was not enough to spank him so his behavior would change. We needed help in understanding what it was that was setting him off.

The class he was in helped him to deal with that. Sometimes his instructor would purposefully allow him to "go over the edge." It was helpful for me to see Nathan do to her what he did to me. Even better, I was able to watch her deal with it. I learned that our instinctive tendencies as moms are not always the best ones! People trained to deal with these behavior problems related to learning difficulties can provide us with significant help. Their techniques work at home as well. I am not too proud to say I simply did not know how to handle my son. I learned, and now emulate their techniques. They certainly work better than mine ever did.

I should qualify the above paragraph by saying that not all diagnoses will be accurate, and not all teachers assigned to your child will be the right ones. This process has to be evaluated by the parents, as is true of any other activity our children take part in. In our situation the Lord revealed the truth through our local speech center and provided just the right people at the right time.

A Word of Encouragement

Tuesday, March 25, 1997, found Katie, Nathan, and me at Vanderbilt University's Child Development Center. We were there to get further help with behavior management. More specifically, we needed insight into what it was in the way our family functioned that was provoking Nathan to the point of temper tantrums and how we could all improve our own communication skills in order to prevent these episodes from happening.

The meeting lasted an hour and a half. While Katie and Nathan played at a table with a child psychologist, I observed through a window and was interviewed about how we functioned in our home. After about 45 minutes, the psychologist came in and told me that she thoroughly enjoyed playing with Nathan. But what really impressed her, she said, was Katie. She was surprised by the way that Katie instinctively knew how to communicate with her baby brother and how helpful she had been in the session. She laughed and said that she would love to have Katie's help with her other students.

I sheepishly explained that we were a homeschooling family (unsure of how this revelation would be accepted), and that the reason Katie worked so well with Nathan was because she was with him so much. I told her that Katie had struggled with a learning difficulty herself, assuming that the psychologist would have picked up on that during her session with Nathan. She looked surprised and said she did not detect anything that indicated Katie had ever had trouble. She thought that Katie was, in fact, incredibly mature for her age. I, of course, was thrilled! Based on what she observed that day, the psychologist said that she was pleased that we had chosen to homeschool Nathan as well.

I am encouraged that we made wise decisions in getting help for the children when we realized there were problems that we did not have the expertise to deal with alone. There is no shame or lack of faith in realizing that you don't have all the answers and calling upon the help of trained professionals. All children go through predictable developmental milestones at certain ages. If children who have difficulty with language or other developmental issues receive the help they need early, preferably in the preschool years, it is a great advantage to them later. Usually if you wait until later when they have already developed patterns that need to be unlearned, you are in for a struggle.

I realize that the intervention I am writing in support of may seem to conflict with the "better late than early" philosophy (e.g., Raymond and Dorothy Moore) that many homeschooling families have adopted. But it need not be seen as an either/or. Our family embraces both intervention and later education. I fully endorse a lifestyle of learning that is paced by my child's individual readiness. Waiting is not a problem for our family, and we have benefited from the practice. But for children who are not developing normally, I strongly encourage early intervention.

The sessions of intervention are tailored to your child's specific area of need. These sessions are brief compared to the lifelong benefits you will gain from the lessons learned. Parents are given support and are encouraged to observe the lessons so that there is continuity at home and at "school." For instance, when the teacher was trying to increase Nathan's vocabulary, it was time in our homeschool to introduce verbs—more specifically, those with "ing" endings. I got help from Katie and Will in introducing verbs even into the children's playtime! I have also started a personal library for Nathan by obtaining the books read to him during his sessions. He is so delighted by the familiarity of a recognized book pulled out as a treat during our bedtime stories. The teacher at the learning center can tell a difference from the work that is being done at home. In no way does this process interfere with our home education but, in fact, serves to enhance it.

The Homeschool Advantage

Getting help with learning difficulties was a wise decision for us. But the decision that I think has been most important in seeing our children develop is the decision to homeschool. There are marvelous advantages to homeschooling your child, but these advantages are magnified when it comes to teaching a child who has learning difficulties. The most fundamental advantage is that they get more one-on-one time with a loving parent who is willing to tailor their education to their specific needs. This is certainly not possible in the normal classroom setting.

It became obvious at one point that the subject which we most needed to concentrate on was language arts. So during the summer months one year, we put all other subjects aside while Katie read some 20 readers out loud and then narrated the stories back to me, while I typed her reports into the computer. We worked on reading skills, comprehension, and grammar. It proved to be a most productive summer. To encourage the fine motor skills needed to improve her writing, Katie and I began sewing together. Now, at age ten, she surprises Michael and me with hand-embroidered samplers that she has designed herself. Her stitches are amazing, and she really enjoys this creative outlet.

Not only can homeschool parents tailor education to the needs of their children, but they can also protect them from the ridicule and rejection that can so injure self-confidence. Children with learning difficulties require more steps to reach the heights, while others seem to leap the hurdles so easily. But at home their work is not compared with that of other children, nor are they criticized because it takes them a little longer to get it. They can be encouraged without being rushed. I can now say with great satisfaction that, if anything, Katie is actually a little overconfident. But I would much rather have to "rein in" overconfidence than have to attempt to build confidence by working out of the mire of inner disbelief.

Protecting our children from humiliation or public disgrace does not mean that we are pampering them. They are required to learn the same rules as any other child and obey them. We just have to teach them differently. Nathan's teacher designed a "rule board" for us that hangs on our refrigerator. It has pictures on it to remind us of the rules: No screaming. No hitting. No throwing. If you don't listen, time-out! Nathan has proudly memorized these rules and takes them very seriously. One day, when Will spilled a cup of milk all over the floor, Michael raised his voice. "Will!" he yelled, "what are you doing?"

Nathan calmly assessed the situation and produced a verdict: "Daddy, the rule says 'no yelling,' so you will have to sit in time-out!"

All the hugs and kisses in the world will not console Nathan when he is angry, nor should they. He wants to be understood, and I want him to act responsibly. Therefore, the child with learning problems is not pampered, and the rules do not change. They are just enforced differently.

Another advantage to homeschooling is the influence the child with learning difficulties and his siblings can have on each other. Brothers and sisters learn to avoid self-preoccupation because they are called to become helpers to Mom and Dad in working with the child who is having trouble. The siblings actually become teachers themselves and benefit from being needed within the family. I have often resisted compliments from people who have said, "You are doing such a good job with Nathan!" and pointed their compliments toward Will. Will has taught Nathan more than I ever could through the way they play. Boys simply play differently than girls, and Will has had the hours to spend inviting and encouraging Nathan to play. This playtime has fed his imagination, increased his vocabulary, encouraged him to relate to a playmate peaceably, and developed a deep friendship in the meantime. It teaches him to be part of a team and to control his temper while playing games like basketball. Had Will been away at school, their friendship and love for one another would not be nearly so intimate or life-changing.

The home environment is the best one for keeping an eye on our children's progress. We are with them in all situations, so we can be quick to evaluate what is working and what is not working. We then have the freedom to change the way we teach material or the speed at which we are working, or to ask for help from others within the community. If we are doing a good job of listening, we know when our child is in trouble.

The advantages are not only for the child. They are for the parents as well. The work may be harder, but the rewards are greater. Nathan has a "listen to me" language he learned from his teacher, Ms. Lisa. He will come to me when he has something he really wants to communicate and will take my face in his little hands, turning it toward his. He will hold it there until he's through speaking.

One night as I tucked him into bed, Nathan grabbed my face and held it in front of his own. "Listen to me," he instructed. "I your boy and you are my girl."

"Oh, Nathan, you are so sweet," I said as I tried to kiss his cheek. He held my face once more in his little hands and very authoritatively said in a slow and awkward speech, "Listen! Listen to me! I love you and you love me!" I was surprised by joy. I held my son close, absorbing his words. He didn't understand the tears trickling down my face, so he got up to get me a cup of water in order to make me feel better. It is a feeling beyond description when you have loved someone beyond your grasp for so long, and they finally are able to communicate to you what you have so much longed to hear. Not just that he loves me, but that he knows I love him.

Teaching a child with difficulties can be like running a marathon. For so long you just run and run, the ribbon out of your range of sight. Finally a moment comes when you catch sight of the goal and eventually you break through it.

Somehow the race means so much more because it required so much more effort.

Resources

If you have questions or concerns as to whether your own slow learner has developmental problems, your most accessible resource is your own pediatrician. He or she can direct you to centers that conduct learning evaluations should you or your pediatrician become suspicious that there is a problem. Usually the pediatrician will conduct hearing tests and screenings for child development during the annual physical. This is a great time to voice concerns and ask questions.

Another resource for help may be the public school system. If your insurance will not help cover the cost of your sessions, they can get very expensive. The public school system is required to give help to children with learning difficulties free of charge. The center that tested our children indicated that they would act as a liaison for us if we wanted them to. I have avoided this route because I did not want to get tied up with the school system. Plus, the mothers that I sit with during class say it is a constant battle to defend your child and what your child needs. Because the school system provides free care, they have to screen carefully who gets what service and may not evaluate your child's needs to your liking. Be prepared for a series of exhausting meetings to plead your case if you decide to go this direction.

There is also an organization for homeschoolers called NATHHAN. I have not used it for the simple reason that I am getting what I need for now. But I have talked to many people who have indicated that this is a very helpful resource. The address is:

National Challenged Homeschoolers
Associated Network
5383 Alpine Road SE
Olaua, WA 98359
Phone number: (206) 857-4257

From Susan's journal—March 1996:

This warm, breezy spring morning found Michael and me swinging on the front porch talking about Nathan and the unique perspective he brings. I had just come down from the tree house. I had been observing the blossoms on the poplar trees that bloom too high to see from the ground. "You know," Michael began, "the way to think of Nathan is like the poplars. Some trees bloom high, and you have to wait to see the blossoms when they fall from the tree." I embrace that thought. Some trees bloom high.

Michael's Perspective
Learning Enablers

The Lord has blessed us—yes, *blessed* us—with two "special needs" children. Before they were in our lives, we would assure and comfort parents who were similarly blessed. But our sympathy came from nothing more than head knowledge. Now, because of our own experiences, Susan and I can affirm with the certainty of heart and mind that the Lord works wonderful things through the frailties and fragility of special children.

Katie's hurdle was relatively small. It involved her speech and the way she understood words and put sentences together. She is basically past her problem and continues to mature normally (whatever that is).

Nate's problem, so far as we can tell now, is more severe. Though he is now four, his speech lags well behind that of his three-year-old sister. Beyond all that, his overall ability to communicate seems stilted and stunted. For a father who specializes in communicating, this has been a wonderful challenge.

Years ago, late one evening, I was watching the moon rise over the poplars that surround our house. There was a dim light in the room behind me, and all at once something happened that was so ordinary and yet so remarkable that I've been pondering it ever since.

I looked through the window and saw the pale crest of the moon in the trees and in the same instant the light behind me reflected my own image in the same window. It was both a window to see through and a mirror to see by, all at once.

It was, of course, an ordinary, everyday experience, seeing your face and the moon. And yet at the same time, I was looking in two directions at once, both outward and inward. That experience has somehow shaped the way I look at the world in general and at my special children in particular.

Their fragility forces me to slow down, to explain or communicate as well as listen to their frequently fragmented attempts to tell. This slowing-down helps me see the world in a new way, from a fresh perspective. I look through their lives as I would a window and out onto a transformed landscape where small things matter: bugs and rocks and dew on grass. I often catch myself listening to myself explain otherwise simple concepts to them, all the while coming to a new and deeper understanding myself of whatever it is. They frame the world for me. I have now, as N.C. Wyeth said of his children, "four live contacts with life instead of only my own." This is all a wonderful part of the blessing of special children, and indeed of all children. They are windows through which we see the world: fresh, innocent, and new.

As well as being windows we can see through, our children can also become mirrors in which we see ourselves. When Katie was struggling with words, I was able, through my compassion for her, to find some new and much-needed compassion for myself. For in my own way I struggle with those "clumsy bricks" as much as she. When I hold Nate during one of the angry outbursts which are a symptom of his disability, I see the anger in myself, but I also see myself as marvelously "held." The truth is, to one degree or another, we are all handicapped. It is just that some handicaps are more visible than others. And while I am looking out at a new landscape through the windows that are my children, I, at the same instant, look at the "inscape" of my own life in a new and holier way.

To experience life anew, what greater gift is there? To have the cluttered landscape of your life made clean and fresh—what more could you ask for? To have blind eyes opened to see and deaf ears unstopped to hear the music that God ceaselessly performs through creation—that is, I believe, the purpose behind the pain of what we so wrongfully refer to as "handicaps." Because, if the truth be known, they are not disabilities because they do not disable. Rather, they enable in new and marvelous ways. At least they can, if we will allow God's great and tender grace to work in the midst of them.

SEVEN

Companions on the Journey

Listening to Your Child's Uniqueness

ℒisten to the sacred silence
Listen to the Holy Word
Listen as He speaks through living
Parables that must be heard

Lyric from "Will You Not Listen?"/*The Word*
Words and Music by Michael Card
Used by permission

*A*s companions to our children on their journey through life, we are responsible to see that they have the necessary provisions. It is a bit like preparing for a long mountain climb. In packing a backpack for a difficult hike, you need to make certain that you have the specific items that will be needed for the arduous journey which lies ahead. Without the proper provisions, your trip will be more difficult and, perhaps, unsuccessful. Just as we must take great care in packing for such a journey, so much more do we need to make sure our children have what they need for their journey into adulthood—a journey that will take a lifetime to complete. To help them along this path, we must ask ourselves several questions:

What direction are we going?
What are the strengths we can impart to our
    children?
What are the personal weaknesses we have that
    require us to call on other people for help?
What resources are available to us now, and will they
    be available further down the pike?

We must take careful inventory to achieve what Ken Gire has called "the most rigorous of disciplines—the discipline of awareness." I so much appreciate the honesty he shows in admitting the difficulty of this important facet of spiritual and personal growth.

This "discipline of awareness" is a must for parents who are committed to walking with Christ. That commitment to the Lord will help us make the right choices in our own lives and the lives of our children. These choices should flow out of the relationship we have with our heavenly Father. But that doesn't mean that they are easy. We are so often tempted toward the easy and the expedient. We must choose the right path, in spite of its difficulty. We can either lounge about at the base of the mountain looking upward, denying what lies before us, or we can brace ourselves for the task and prepare to make the breathtaking climb. Once we have committed ourselves to the journey, we must really learn the art of listening, for this is the key to developing the needed awareness.

Learning to Listen

It was in college that I first learned about the challenge of listening. One chilly autumn night, my professor, Dr. Bill Lane, and his wife, Brenda, were giving me a ride back to my dormitory after we had attended a church service together. We had been riding in silence for some time. The only sound was the rain on the windows and the slapping rhythm of the windshield wipers. I was reflecting on the sermon and the challenge it had presented: to live a godly life, one that is set apart from a nonbelieving world. I shared with Bill and Brenda my disappointment with the fact that Christians on campus did not act any differently than non-Christians. There did not seem to be much to distinguish the two.

As he pulled up to the door to drop me off, Bill looked over his shoulder and said, "Well, Susan, the difference between the Christian and the non-Christian is that the Christian is the one who adopts a lifestyle of listening." His eyebrows were raised above his glasses and his eyes direct as he spoke these words aloud. He left me on the pavement that night searching my heart and mind for what he meant by those few choice words. This chapter reflects some of the conclusions I've reached about this very deep truth. For this "lifestyle of listening" means that we must attune our hearts to hear the voice of God in the variety of ways that it comes to us.

Listening to the Word

> Now choose life, so that you and your children may live and that you may love the LORD your God, listen to his voice, and hold fast to him (Deuteronomy 30:19-20).

We can either walk through life on solid ground, or we can muddle around in quicksand. I have done a little of both, and definitely prefer solid ground! It is a firm grounding in truth that gives us the stability to respond to all we face in life. Scripture answers the question, "What direction should we take?" It is a living book, which translates truth into the context of our daily lives. Without truth, the choices we must make as to how we live our lives are left to experimentation. But instead of leaving it to ourselves to figure out, we should be working with the master plan already laid out by the Creator Himself. That master plan is found in the Word of God. It is a provision for our life's journey, a covering, and a source of wisdom. It reaches into our personal lives and into the way our home functions. By listening intently to the Word of God, we become acquainted with the master plan, finding within it much freedom for exploration and insight. Without it, you are a traveler lost and disoriented on the byways of life. With the Word of God, you are a traveler with a map or a navigator with a compass.

Our first objective as travelers, then, is to obtain the guidebook and search it to find discernment as we encounter a world filled with propaganda. We must combat lies with truth, *the* truth. The purpose of understanding truth is to embrace the wisdom we need "for giving prudence to the simple, knowledge and discretion to the young" (Proverbs 1:4). Truth engages us in a lifestyle that equips us for life. This lifestyle of engaging our hearts and minds with the Word is called a devotional lifestyle. It is a path we must follow our whole lives long. It is a misconception to think that once we are adults we are no longer in need of educating ourselves. "Let the wise listen and add to their learning, and let the discerning get guidance" (Proverbs 1:5). We are to live our days interacting with the Lord through reading Scripture, listening to wisdom, and then applying it to our lives. "Do not merely listen to the word, and so deceive yourselves. Do what it says" (James 1:22). Only then do we have life-giving truth to pass on to our children.

God's Image-bearers

> Then God said, "Let us make man in our image, in our likeness . . ." (Genesis 1:26).

This particular Scripture reference is a good place to begin when reflecting on who we are. In the broadest sense, man is made in the image of God. But that, of course, doesn't mean we're all alike. God creates each of us to be unique. No one person is exactly like another. When we think of how many of God's "image-bearers" have existed from the beginning to the present time, and how many people have populated the earth, it causes us to ponder again the mystery of God's greatness. How can so many unique individuals all be created in God's image? If this is true, then He is vast and complex indeed.

Because we are all created to bear God's image in a unique manner, there is so much that we can learn from one another. From our living brothers and sisters. From those saints who have preceded us. Even from those who set themselves up as the enemies of the gospel. The wise person will learn to listen to the messages of God, no matter who they come from.

Ecclesiastes 3:11 says, "He has also set eternity in the hearts of men." There is a hole in our hearts that only God can fill. There is an awareness of God that is His gift to all people. We should learn to exercise that gift through learning the art of listening.

We all begin in the womb, in "the secret place," hidden from the outside world—a place where the Father creates, knits, makes, and weaves together something fearful and wonderful. And what a wonder it is! As the psalmist writes:

> For you created my inmost being; you knit me together in my mother's womb. I praise you because I am fearfully and wonderfully made; your works are wonderful, I know that full well. My frame was not hidden from you when I was made in the secret place. When I was woven together in the depths of the earth, your eyes saw my unformed body. All the days ordained for me were written in your book before one of them came to be (Psalm 139:13-16).

What an amazing thing it is to hear a baby's first cry and watch as the infant adapts to life outside the womb. His cry is so fierce at first, taking vigorous breaths as his tiny lungs begin to expand with the new responsibility of providing much-needed oxygen. His tiny fists shake, his blood begins to surge as he takes on the color of life. It is truly a wonder and a miracle. My encouragement to you is this: Don't lose sight of the wonder of creation. Never stop looking and listening.

After each of our children was born and we knew they were alive and well, we would immediately turn our focus to their features. "Look at her fingers, they're so long!" "Are his eyes blue, or is that brown I see?" "Oh! She has a dimple in her chin." These were the kind of observations we made. We were always looking for the unique characteristics of each baby. Or we would ask ourselves in what ways our own features or the features of their grandparents translated into this new person.

As our children grew from tiny newborns to toddlers, we were also looking for uniqueness in their dispositions. Were they cheerful, melancholic, withdrawn, aggressive, curious, or disinterested? As time went on, these observations developed into more specific questions. What activity is he attracted to? What is her favorite toy? What picture book does he like the most? Does she like music? There is a seemingly endless list of questions that we ask ourselves in the attempt to answer the larger one: Who are you, my special child? In what ways are you one of God's unique "image-bearers"?

Waiting for these little persons to grow can be an anxious time. It can be so hard to wait! But as we wait for our gardens to grow and blossom, so we must wait for our children. Not one spring goes by that I am not reporting to one of my dear friends the progress of my peonies. They are my favorite flowers. I can give almost daily reports on their progress: when they resurfaced; whether or not the young growth survived the dogs, the lawnmower, and the children; and the delight over how many blossoms we have this year. The excitement mounts when I awaken to the flower opening with its beauty and its sweet fragrance, its own unique characteristics of God's wonderful creation.

So it is with our children. We wait anxiously as they grow physically and in the development of their character. "Who are you?" I think to myself as I watch them go about the different activities of their day. "Who are you going to become?" "What can God teach me through you, and you through me?"

Your Child's Uniqueness

One of the wonderful things Michael and I have enjoyed from our homeschooling experience is how it gives us the opportunity to know our children better. The con-

stant companionship of learning together gives us many opportunities to draw closer to one another. We are able to listen to their lives through the many hours of watching them in their many activities, listening to them as they interact with their world and their studies, and observing how they each respond to us in their own unique ways.

I give much credit to Ken Cope of C.O.R.E. resources (Nashville, Tennessee) and Ralph Mattson of The Doma Group (Minneapolis, Minnesota) for teaching me how to improve my skills of actively listening to my children. They teach that everyone is created by God's design (Psalm 139) to fulfill his or her own purpose. Each of us is gifted in some area. They emphasize that, instead of deciding in advance what we would like our children to be interested in (often to fulfill our own ambitions), we listen closely to learn what our children are interested in.

In a booklet titled *How to Discover Your Child's Unique Gifts,* Ralph Mattson encourages his readers to begin a design journal. A design journal is a place where you can record your observations about each of your children. This has become a habit with me. Because nonverbal communication makes up a larger percentage than verbal, we learn best by watching our children's activities. What do they do with their free time? What do they say while they are doing it? Mattson also encourages his reader to have their children tell stories. This has been particularly interesting to me, for it opens new windows on understanding my children. The insights I have gained from this activity have helped me to be realistic in my expectations of them. They also help determine how I tell them to do a task.

To keep such a journal may seem like an overwhelming task, but it is not. You simply jot things down in your journal over a period of a few weeks or months. You'll quickly see recurring themes in their behavior, attitudes, and interests.

The recurring themes in Katie's journal were often about details. In telling stories back to me, I began to realize that, though she was unaware of the larger concept in an event or an activity, she remembered many details. Precision was important to her. Even though she may not always complete every task, the precision she brings to her performance of each aspect of it is incredible. She learns from the bottom up. She stacks facts to come to the conclusion of the whole, like building a tower block by block. With activities like cleaning her room, we often come to a frustrated end when I say, "Katie, go clean your room." This concept seems vast and intangible for her. Instead, I have learned that I need to define what cleaning her room means. I need to be specific: Make your bed, arrange your pillows, pick up the clothes on the floor, fold them and put them in your dresser, put your toys in their special box, let me know when you are finished. When I use this method to tell her to clean her room, we meet with great success.

Will is completely different. He learns from the large concept and extracts truth from it. What is interesting about Will's learning process is that he is very verbal. He loves to talk! For him to really learn something, he needs to talk it through. When Will tells me stories about activities, he does not mention the details. Instead, he talks about the people involved. His eyes widen and his voice gets excited. If he went to the zoo, he would tell me who was there and what they said. If Katie went to the zoo, she would not mention the people, but would note the fact that the Siberian tiger weighed 700 pounds!

This knowledge of my children is intriguing, important, and helpful. Had they not been schooled at home, I might have missed much about these uniquenesses, for it is in the learning situation that much of this comes out. I would have had to base my knowledge on what different teachers had to say. I much prefer doing the observations myself and getting to know my children in this deeper way.

This knowledge is also an advantage to them. Katie is already aware of her need to break things down into details. Will needs a lot of social time, so we began participating in Cub Scouts. Nathan needs to learn to adjust to changes without getting upset. Maggie at age three has me full of suspicions, but still incomplete conclusions. But by listening and observing, I'll continue to learn about her needs and gifts. For all my children, I desire to provide freedom to exercise the gifts God has given them and, as Mattson encourages us, accept them for who they are!

Learning Styles

Because we are all unique, we all have different learning styles, different ways we take in and absorb information. Michael learns best by trial and error; I learn best by following a sequential order. The way we learn affects the way we teach. When I study to prepare lessons for the children, I will look for outlines and charts to help me grasp how the information holds together. When reading about Augustine, for example, I drew out a time line of the events of his life. It helped me to organize the material in my mind and for my presentation.

Even though this is the most natural method for me, that does not always mean it will be the best for my children. Sometimes I have to change my approach to meet their learning styles. Cynthia Ulrich Tobias has written two very helpful books on learning styles. *The Way They Learn* and *Every Child Can Succeed* help explain the different styles and how best to tailor your teaching toward your child's dominant style. But as helpful as this method is, don't allow yourself to get too bogged down in finding the right "label" for your children. No child perfectly fits into the mold for any one kind of learner. No one category fully describes any child. We have traits that overlap because we are not simple creatures. Tobias admits that all of us are too complicated to be pegged as having one particular personality trait or learning style. Listen to your child and learn how you can best help him or her as a unique individual.

Because Katie is what Tobias calls a "random thinker," I encourage the use of narration as a method of making sure that she has comprehended the material. I want her to be able to repeat back to me what the story is about. When Katie is doing her math, I have to teach her to resist the temptation to work randomly all over the page. She has to learn to do her math in its proper order if she is to prevent making lots of mistakes. On other assignments, like journaling, I allow her randomness free rein to express itself.

Michael is an explorer when it comes to learning. He must travel the path himself if he is to really learn something. When he teaches the kids, he is not excited about using textbooks. Instead, he likes to digest the information for himself and then teach it to the children in his own words. He teaches as someone who has already traveled the path and is now a trail guide.

All of us are unique, and an understanding of our uniqueness can make us better learners, as well as better teachers.

Help from Others

There are wonderful resources all around us for teaching our children. We cannot ignore the rich opportunities that we have. We must introduce our children to what the community around them has to offer and help them to sift through what is helpful, and discern what is not.

Taking field trips is an excellent way to introduce them to the wider world. For homeschoolers, field trips can be based upon everyday activities. There is much to learn all around us. A trip to the library can teach children how to browse quietly. (It is also an occasion for you to see what they gravitate toward.) Special trips to a bakery, a printing office, a working farm—any of these add exposure to what makes our communities work. More important is the resource of the people in our lives. Our pastors, neighbors, friends, and families all play a role in our child's life. Their observations and insights are worth listening to.

Our church community is also a helpful source of strength and guidance. Here our children learn the ways of the Lord and how to worship Him in a community setting. Although Sunday school alone is not adequate to teach our children what they need to know of the Bible and the Christian life, it can provide another teacher to reinforce the message.

Finally, we should take advantage of the resources of other homeschooling families. Coffees, discussion groups, books, magazines, even e-mail, can become ways of sharing important information or providing much-needed encouragement. But sometimes there are so many voices saying so many different things that it can be confusing. My best advice is to get involved in a small support group of like-minded homeschooling parents. Learn by asking others, pool resources, share talents and gifts, and help one another to make wise choices. Whatever struggles you might be facing, it is likely that others have had to deal with the same difficulties. Their experiences may help you not to make any unnecessary mistakes!

Michael's Perspective
A Lifestyle of Listening

The framework for who I am as a Christian man was largely constructed during weekly walks with Bill Lane, my mentor from university days. Though I was in my early twenties, he could walk me into the ground and seemed to enjoy doing so—twice around campus at a breakneck pace, rain or snow or shine. I vividly remember one time when the snow piled up on his great bushy eyebrows.

There were a few phrases Bill repeated again and again. They were his special discoveries, made over a lifetime of listening to his own life. He repeated them endlessly, or so it seemed to me. One of his favorites was, "Timing is of the Lord." That was his response to, among many others, my agonizing questions about whom I would marry and when. Another prhase he loved to bellow with a booming voice as he strolled around the classroom, handing out another nearly impossible test was, "*Lo rachamim!*" (no mercy). Even now I can taste the fear in my mouth at the sound of those mischievous words.

"Let it simmer on the back burner of your mind," he would say when we would talk about some prospective topic for a paper. I found it was indeed true. When I was perplexed by some exegetical problem, I would often go to sleep with it "simmering," only to wake with the solution.

One of his common phrases still simmers on the back burner of my mind. "You must develop a lifestyle of listening," he would often say when we would speak about some difficulty I was having with some person or another. "The best way to show someone you love them is by listening," he said once on one of our walks. Twenty-five years later I have finally begun to understand the wisdom of those words. That's a long time to simmer!

The best way we can show our children our love is by listening to them. Susan has taught me this powerfully from her example. When it comes to our children, she is a great listener. Not only does she listen to their words, but to their silences as well. One of the first things we must learn as listeners is that children, as well as adults, often don't mean what they say. This makes becoming a listener even more challenging.

The ability to demonstrate love by true listening is one of the greatest pluses of a homeschool education. Many times, due to overcrowding and lack of time, other educational systems can become a "dialogue of the deaf." The teachers speak without really listening either to the students or themselves. But within the freeing confines of home we have the greatest opportunities to listen to our children's lives and hear most clearly what they need and who they are.

We need to nurture in our children the ability to truly listen. To help them become listeners is to convince them that the best way to show others you love them is to listen to them. And those others include God Himself. If indeed we truly love Him, we will listen to Him, listen for Him. For He speaks to us in His Word and in prayer as we silence our hearts.

EIGHT

Feeding the Mind

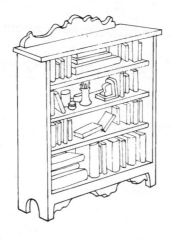

So many books, so little time
So many hunger, so many blind
Starving for words, they must wait in the night
To open a Bible and move towards the Light

Lyric from "So Many Books . . ."/*The Word*
Words and Music by Michael Card
Used by permission

I have spent the last seven chapters discussing issues which are closely related to feeding the hearts of your children. Now in this chapter let's look at the importance of academics—the feeding of the mind. Some will undoubtedly question why I have put off this discussion so long. Why not give priority to the question of academic excellence? After all, are not academics the foundation of education? Simply put, the answer is no. I think that the most biblical position is to strike a balance between these two areas. A friend recently informed me that when he did a word study from the Bible on the words *heart* and *mind*, there were more references to issues of the heart than of the mind.

Without a doubt there is a need for us all to gain knowledge and understanding. The better educated we are, the more intellectual resources we have to offer our communities. Our knowledge and experience can open up more opportunities for finding meaningful employment and the financial stability this brings. Therefore, our academic studies are a critical aspect of the homeschooling decision. Parents know the importance of a well-rounded education—one that will prepare our children to be experts in the particular field they may choose to embrace for their future careers. There is no question that academic excellence is important. But it is not the only thing, or even necessarily the most important!

Our resolve to keep our children home for their education was a way to express our belief that matters of the heart have precedence over matters of the mind. We can stuff our minds full of facts, but if we do not engage the heart in the process, then our education is unbalanced and will leave us ill-equipped to face moral and social issues. We need more than just knowledge. We need wisdom.

Our approach to education, then, should be one that integrates the heart and the mind. This embodies true understanding. Our children need to be nurtured, to be raised and trained with all areas of development taken into consideration. And this nurturing does not take place only in the preschool years. It is a continual process. Eventually, the need to be nurtured will mature into the need to be discipled and mentored. Our children need individualized attention. The lack of such time spent in a nurturing relationship is evident in the lives of children across our nation, taking the form of emotional starvation, rebellion, and destruction. Our children need our time if they are to grow in wisdom—that unique blending of the heart and the mind.

In his book *A Third Testament*, Malcolm Muggeridge gives us a fine example of how wisdom can have a profound influence on our personal lives and on our culture. Muggeridge tells the story of six great men, all of whom he refers to as "God's spies." Augustine, Blaise Pascal, William Blake, Soren Kierkegaard, Leo Tolstoy, and Dietrich Bonhoeffer are all men who shared a common purpose given to them by God. As spies, they remained somewhat inconspicuous, blending with the enemy-occupied territory of their place and time. But God used them in powerful ways to demonstrate His own wisdom. These were men who fit in, but had the wisdom of the heart and intelligence of the mind to make a lasting impact on their world. In the Scriptures, we see this same powerful combination in the prophet Daniel. It would be hard to find a better example of what we hope to accomplish in homeschooling.

Daniel was a learned man, but one who did not forsake his convictions. When Nebuchadnezzar, the king of Babylon, took the nation of Israel in captivity, he ordered his chief officials to bring some Israelites into the royal court. Specifically, he wanted "young men without any physical defect, handsome, showing aptitude for every kind of learning, well informed, quick to understand, and qualified to serve in the king's palace" (Daniel 1:4). They were to learn the language and literature of the Babylonians. Daniel was chosen to be one of these young men. He showed himself quick to learn the language and literature of the Babylonians, but this did not mean that he had to abandon the convictions of his heart.

The king assigned the sumptuous food and drink from his own table to be given to his new pupils, along with the best possible education. Thus prepared, they would become the king's special servants. Daniel declined the sumptuous feast, but he did not decline the education. God showed favor on Daniel and the other young men. "To these four young men God gave knowledge and understanding of all kinds of literature and learning. And Daniel could understand visions and dreams of all kinds" (Daniel 1:17). These men became so well educated and demonstrated such wisdom that even outsiders respected them.

> At the end of the time set by the king to bring them in, the chief official presented them to Nebuchadnezzar. The king talked with them, and he found none equal to Daniel, Hananiah, Mishael and Azariah; so they entered the king's service. In every matter of wisdom and understanding about which the king questioned them, he found them ten times better than all the magicians and enchanters in his whole kingdom (Daniel 1:18-20).

Note that Daniel, though possessing an excellent education, still relied on God to reveal truth.

Later, when Nebuchadnezzar had a troubling dream, Daniel was able to demonstrate a wisdom beyond that of the astrologers and wise men of the king's court. He knew who to turn to for the revelation of truth: God. "Then Daniel returned to his house and explained the matter to his friends. . . . He urged them to plead for mercy from the God of heaven concerning this mystery. . . . During the night the mystery was revealed to Daniel in a vision" (Daniel 2:17-19). Daniel, with a grateful heart, praised God before he went to help the king.

Daniel is a good example for our need to be grounded in God-given wisdom, as well as academic study. His life exposes our need for God to be the revealer of truth and the provider of wisdom. We may sometimes be like "God's spies," camouflaged for a period of time, only to win the respect of the world in the end by demonstrating the wisdom of God.

But the Lord does not limit His call to only the well-educated. He uses both the faithful and the unfaithful, the learned and the unlearned, to fulfill His purposes. A man or woman of faithfulness, regardless of educational background, may be called upon to stand out among the people and serve God. Remember what happened when God spoke to Moses from the burning bush and told him to approach Pharaoh?

> Moses said to the LORD, "O Lord, I have never been eloquent, neither in the past nor since you have spoken to your servant. I am slow of speech and tongue." The LORD said to him, "Who gave man his mouth? Who makes him deaf or mute? Who gives him sight or makes him blind? Is it not I, the LORD? Now go; I will help you speak and will teach you what to say" (Exodus 4:10-12).

Therefore, we must approach the question of academics prayerfully. We need to teach our children to rely on God in this area of their lives as well, to see their studies as part of their obedience to God. Academics can sometimes cause us to feel inadequate. But the Lord can and will use our inadequacies. We have a tremendous resource in what the Lord will do. Parents who are willing to apply themselves can teach their children the art of learning.

What Is Your Philosophy of Education?

If someone asked you, "What is your philosophy of education?" would you be able to give them an answer? Have you ever really thought about what your goals are in teaching your children at home? These are important questions to ask yourself. There are many different approaches to schooling at home, each with many loyal adherents. If you are to find the one that works best for your family, you'll need to do some exploring. I suggest that you spend some time reading about the different points of view. For example, *For the Children's Sake* by Susan Schaeffer Macaulay is an excellent introduction to Charlotte Mason and her natural approach to learning. You might also want to read *Recovering the Lost Tools of Learning* by Douglas Wilson, to get some insights on a traditional classical form of education. I found *Dumbing Us Down* by John Taylor Gatto to be helpful for getting an inside view of the problems in our public school system. *Better Late than Early* by Raymond and Dorothy Moore has been popular with many families. Read these and other books, and allow yourself to be challenged. Sometimes we reach our own personal philosophy by finding what we disagree with, as much as learning from what we find agreeable.

Everyone needs to be able to articulate his or her philosophy. Fortunately, Michael and I are fairly like-minded in our approach, though we differ in how we implement it. I believe it is very healthy for children to experience different educational styles. So on occasion, Michael teaches the entire day. He follows the curriculum outline that I am working with, but he uses his own unique teaching style. I have found that Michael is helpful in balancing my perspective and in helping me to remain balanced. And *balance* has become a key term in articulating our educational philosophy.

I have found that I need balance in order to face long days as both a mother and a teacher. I apply this same balance to my philosophy of education. We have sought to find the balance between early intervention and the Moores' "better late than early" approach. We balance the need for routine with the willingness to be spontaneous. We balance workbook exercises with real-life experiences.

When we began homeschooling, I found that there were two things I needed to do. First, I had to embrace the responsibility of researching the options and choosing a curriculum. (A mentor like Valerie can be a great help in this process!) Then I had to evaluate how these curriculum choices actually worked within the variables of our family's situation. Consequently, I have made many adjustments to better meet the needs of my children. Because the educational process is an interactive one, we cannot afford to sit by passively, assuming our goals are being accomplished. We must monitor our progress, along with the attitudes of our children, and see if our goals are being met.

Our philosophy on education is to approach the learning environment in a "listening" posture. As teachers of our children, we seek to observe, evaluate, research, and respond in order to reach our goals. Here are some of the goals we have set for ourselves:

- To seek the Lord above all else, loving Him with all of our hearts, with all of our souls, and with all of our minds

- To build and maintain character that is Christ-centered in nature and reveals itself through spiritual growth and good citizenship

- To protect the children from influences that would defeat or interfere with our goals

- To develop and maintain a posture of listening that would foster independent studies based on the children's interests

- To teach accurately and thoroughly the core subjects: Bible, character building, language arts, English, literature, mathematics, history, geography, science and nature, health and safety, physical education, and any other extracurricular subjects we feel are necessary for an excellent education

- To facilitate, within our means, any further studies our children wish to specialize in

- To expose our children to a wide range of differing cultures

- To teach the children how to be resourceful

- To be aware of our teaching style in the context of the children we are teaching, and to teach, when possible, in a format they are better able to understand

- To listen to our children as they communicate who they are and to respect God's design for their individuality

- To provide tools and life experiences to enrich their education

- To nurture as best we can their interests and develop their love for learning

- To be ready and willing to place our children in a different educational environment if need be

These goals illlustrate our educational philosophy. You would, no doubt, express yours in a somewhat different manner. The important thing is to take the time to think through what our goals are. If we, as parents, do not know what we want to accomplish, we will probably not achieve the best educational experience for our children. If we don't decide what we want, then the government will be happy to decide for us!

The Subject Matter

Part of having a balanced educational approach is to keep in balance all the many subjects which we need to introduce to our children. Each one plays a role in developing their character and giving them the tools they need for intellectual maturity.

Bible

Studying Scripture devotionally should start as soon as our children are able to listen. It can be as simple as singing scriptural lullabies in the rocking chair or teaching them the names of the various parts of God's creation, all with the goal of transitioning them into a living relationship with Jesus. Repetition is the best approach to early learning from the Bible.

We have read through the entire Bible in storybook form seven times already, learning new details each time we read through. Now that we are reading straight from the Bible, we are adding another level that reaches deeper into the revelation of who God is and what our relationship to Him can become. The goal in teaching the Bible is to introduce them to the Lord, to teach them to recognize His unique voice, and to encourage them in their personal walk with Him.

We have also added the aspect of studying the Bible historically. To study Scripture historically is to give color to the text by grasping the "life situation." We learn to ask the question, "What was life like at that time?" This involves biblical geography, looking at maps in order to locate the regions mentioned. It involves creating or following time-lines in order to memorize the sequence of events. It involves integrating secular texts with biblically based texts to see God's hand in all of history. It involves becoming familiar with the laws and customs of the day. This approach helps us learn to engage our minds as well as our hearts.

Character Building

Character building is an overflow of our response to God's Word. When we respond in obedience, we begin to change! In this teaching we emphasize the various aspects of a good character. For example, we learn about honesty through reading illustrations of how it was lived out in the lives of others, and then by giving examples of what it looks like in our own real-life situations. It is important for our children to form a visual image of what this or any other attribute "looks" like in action. So we discuss character qualities during the course of the day, whether we are reprimanding the children for doing something wrong or praising them for doing something good. We must interact daily with the attitudes in our home. Even though, like me, the children usually know what they should do, they do not always do the right thing. But our life journey moves forward by applying the eternal values to everyday situations.

Reading/Literature

There are two types of reading that are important to make a part of education: "read-alouds" (books that parents read to their children) and "readers" (books the children can read for themselves).

Reading aloud is the earliest and most essential form of the academic process. It is also one of the most natural. It stimulates reasoning skills, sequencing skills, and learning to think in terms of cause and effect. Children will pick up proper language usage by seeing it used well. If we have them narrate back what they've heard, we can also help them develop comprehension skills. The two types of learning that are being addressed during read-aloud time are recessive learning (what the children take in), and expressive learning (what they understood and are able to communicate back to you). Both are important and need to be exercised. Reading aloud is a daily occurrence in our home. Most often, we read together at night before the children go to sleep.

Bedtime is a wonderful time to cuddle up and read together. When the day is over and everyone is more relaxed, we grab a book from the shelves and enjoy it together. It is a time when parents can communicate their own joy in reading by introducing great literature to their children. Giving a dramatic interpretation to the stories being read is a great way for enhancing the moment. Make it fun and exciting for them to listen.

As for our children learning to read, we encouraged them to read as soon as they felt "ready." Learning to read gives the children an opportunity to develop their own interests. Sometimes these interests will overlap with other

subjects. They are learning, but they find such learning to be a joy! In our home, we frequently combine our reading with interests in science and nature. Will likes to read about reptiles and insects, and Katie enjoys books about wolves and otters (and just about any other animal!). Sometimes I will assign them readings from readers, particularly during the period when they are learning to read. Later, when they are reading on their own, I try to correlate some of their reading with the period of history we are studying at the time.

Language Arts

Language arts involves providing our children with the "tools" they need to use and understand the English language. Phonics, spelling, grammar, vocabulary, and handwriting all fall under this category. These subjects are critical because they provide the foundation for becoming effective communicators.

We taught reading using the phonetic or "phonics" approach, and like other people we found this to be very successful.

We did not try to force the children to learn to read, but waited until they were ready, until they wanted to read. When they began asking, "What does this say?" we knew that the time was at hand. Then one day, Will simply stated, "Mom, I want you to teach me to read today!"

We use various workbooks to improve our skills in critical thinking, spelling, and grammar. The children love using workbooks if they are not boring, monotonous, or time-consuming. Choose them carefully, but do not become a slave to them. If you overuse them, you wind up mimicking what goes on in the public schools. So this is an area to discerningly exercise your own personal judgment.

Handwriting

Handwriting is also a part of our curriculum. Not only is it important to be able to write well, but I also see doing this every day as a great exercise in "thinking" neatly and concentrating. My children are not at an age yet where their handwriting is meticulous, but at least they are exercising a conscientiousness in that direction and really enjoy improving their skills.

Writing

Writing is a form of expressive learning. The composition of sentences and paragraphs in the form of reports will show you how well your child is able to apply his or her spelling, grammar, and vocabulary. Some parents have found it helpful to have their children write in a journal every day. Other parents have their chidren do special writing projects like letter writing, making lists, or writing reports. This is an area where I rely greatly on the research of the Moores. We encourage writing, but do not do journal writing every day. We make sure that our curriculum choice is one that definitely covers writing skills, but does not exasperate children who are ten years old and younger.

Other forms of writing we emphasize are dictation, narration, and poetry. Dictation is the exercise of reading a sentence while the children write it down with only auditory instruction and cues. They are responsible to get not only the wording correct, but also the punctuation and spelling. Narration is simply telling back a short story or a section of a story in their own words.

Poetry is one of the areas I find the hardest to "teach." I have found that poetry just happens. It is a creative and emotional overflow and, therefore, hard to force. My rule of thumb for younger children is to keep it very simple. We read poetry aloud and learn by example.

Math

Math can be taught in a number of natural settings. The grocery store, the kitchen, the wood shop, the sewing room, and various games we play all supply us with potential math lessons. However, I do not believe in "learning by osmosis" when it comes to math. These real-life situations are very important for translating the use of mathematics in everyday life. But we also must learn math along with a curriculum that is grade-appropriate for the children. Nothing replaces good old discipline when it comes to learning math!

We have used the Miquon math series and have had great success with the first two books. I follow the outline proposed by Ruth Beechick in her "Three-R" series. First, we work with manipulatives in order to get a visual and tactile experience with numbers. Then we identify the physical groupings with numbers through a mental image. But the abstract thinking she refers to does not occur until later years. The foundation for abstract thinking is years of manipulative and mental-image thinking. I am always amazed by the children's ability to process information mathematically, and I still recommend Miquon with its emphasis on manipulatives.

I found it necessary to switch to Saxon math at the third-grade level in order to teach two children at one time. I really enjoy the variety of applications in these lessons: reading calendars, reading thermometers, counting money, telling time, using lengths of measurement, etc. The lessons are rather time-consuming and repetitive, however, and may not work for everyone. Some people I know only try to do half a lesson each day.

I know some homeschoolers are frustrated with the mostly literary approach to education that is so often emphasized. It does not seem to take into account those students who are inclined to higher math skills. If your child is one of these, I would not hesitate to search out material that will feed their special gift in the area of mathematics.

Science/Nature

Teaching science can be intimidating for many parents, who feel inadequate to the task of imparting this kind of information. But we have found that if it is taught in a natural way, it can be a freeing experience of exploring together. Basic to my teaching of science is the need to develop observation skills.

Look and observe. Have your children write down their observations, draw what they see, or simply share their observations verbally. If they learn nothing more than how to observe, they are well on their way to appreciating and using science in an interactive way. Science can tend to be a subject where students are talked "at" instead of talked "to." But science is more than facts upon facts that need to be memorized! It is learning to see.

Observing nature is at the core of our approach to science. It is a natural interest of our children, and so they enjoy exploring. Will has an impressive bug collection. My younger sister, Valerie, gave us a praying mantis egg sac at our recent Easter get-together. I thought it was just an empty sac that she found in her garden from last year. I realized I was wrong three weeks later when tiny praying mantises were all over my kitchen counter! Thus, school that morning started with science. We gathered the babies, gently putting them in the garden (a little squealing went on, I must admit!). We looked in our resources for pictures and descriptions and referred to Will's bug collection to see a real adult mantis.

I love farm life, and so from my perspective we are at an advantage living in the country. We have raised baby goats and chicks, and are still benefiting from the egg production. Now Katie is in the midst of raising a flock of geese. We take walks nearly every day and learn more than we would learn from any organized field trip!

I can think of no other subject that is so marvelous as science and nature. Exploring all the different ecosystems, the order of the solar system, or the intricacies of microbiology—all these are a window to God's wonders. Michael is an amateur astronomer and delights us all with a close look at the night sky. By day we walk the land, and by night we walk among the stars and planets, always learning about God's created order.

History/Geography

I combine the study of history and geography. We study history with a curriculum that emphasizes a biblical worldview: the relation of man and God throughout history, the results of man's defiance of God's will and the result, what can happen if man will cooperate with God's will—this is the stuff of history. We supplement our topics with grade-appropriate books that have to do with the time period we are studying. But our main focus is on the fact that history is living. The past affects the present, and our present moments can change the future.

Because history can be difficult for children to grasp, we use visual aids whenever possible. Homemade time-lines allow the children to creatively retell history by customizing their studies with their own drawings or stickers. We made our time-lines out of big rolls of freezer paper stretched out to give plenty of room. We also use videos and story tapes as supplements. We are using a curriculum published by Beautiful Feet (see the resource list in the back of this book), which I like because it combines history and literature. I also like the order, the choice of reading material, and the use of a journal composition book.

We have plans to study with the Greenleaf Press curriculum in the next year or two. Greenleaf also combines literature and history. For older grades this combination is especially beneficial as it integrates a number of subjects to-gether. After working through the *Greenleaf Guide to the Old Testament*, which focuses on the history of Israel, we hope to follow the curriculum through ancient Egypt, Greece, Rome, the Medieval period, and beyond, as well as through a healthy dose of American history.

Fine Arts

Music and art are approached much like we approach science: hands on and interactive. Michael thought it was important to begin by teaching the children to understand beauty in its many forms. What is true beauty? This is his foundational question. He will pose the question, "Is this beautiful?" to the children as they randomly dial through different radio stations. "Why or why not?" What he is try-ing to accomplish through simple dialogue is to teach them to interact with their world with a critical eye for beauty. And so when we approach music and art, the question is posed regardless of the musician's or the artist's reputation: Is their work truly beautiful? With that as our basis, we seek to expose our children to fine art in books, magazines, mu-seums, posters, and videos. We listen to a wide variety of musical styles.

The fine arts also include drama and dance. Katie par-ticipates in ballet because she wants to, not because I think every girl should. But I do think most children should ex-perience the beauty of Tchaikovsky's *Nutcracker* ballet at least once! Watching musicals on video can provide a great combination of music and dance. We are currently being exposed to Irish dancing through the video *Riverdance*.

To study the arts is to open oneself to the creative spices of life. In their various combinations, the arts produce unique and creative flavors that represent the different peoples across the globe.

Latin

I strongly recommend a classical language study for your children. The study of Latin provides an academic advantage that translates into all other subjects. Through Latin one can obtain a better appreciation and understanding of the English language. It also provides a strong foundation to learn other foreign languages. The study of Latin helps us to reach far back into our historical roots to see who we are and where some of our cultural influences come from.

I recently reviewed a potential science curriculum and found that much of the vocabulary was in Latin. To a young mind, these long technical words can seem meaningless and intimidating. There is nothing appealing about lengthy vocabulary words that come with a string of hard definitions! But if you look at the words through eyes trained in Latin and Greek root words, the intimidation dissipates. Instead of seeing *photosynthesis*, the child sees photo-syn-thesis. Because he or she understands the root words, the child is able to break down the definition into its parts.

We are using the textbook *English from the Roots Up* by Joegil Lundquist (Literacy Unlimited). This is a great presentation of Greek and Latin root words. We began when Katie was in second grade and Will in first in order to get into the "habit" of Latin. We use the cards like flash cards and learn a new root every week in the same way you would learn English vocabulary. Each card is color-coded to signify Greek or Latin and has different examples of words in our vocabulary printed on the back, along with definitions. At this point it requires very little time and reaps great rewards. We also have other Latin resources for further down the pike, and several people have offered their assistance if necessary.

All these subjects join together to help us learn about ourselves, our world, and the God who created us. They feed both our hearts and our minds, helping us to become truly wise people. Is not this what God wants for us? Is not this what we want for our children?

> Praise be to the name of God for ever and ever; wisdom and power are his. He changes times and seasons; he sets up kings and deposes them. He gives wisdom to the wise and knowledge to the discerning. He reveals deep and hidden things; he knows what lies in darkness, and light dwells with him. I thank and praise you, O God of my fathers: You have given me wisdom and power, you have made known to me what we asked of you, you have made known to us the dream of the king (Daniel 2:20-23).

Michael's Perspective
The Discipline of Browsing

"You must develop a browsing discipline," Dr. Lane once said as he recounted his adventures in the basement of the Harvard Library. There he would "browse" through the archaeological dig reports, reading the inscriptions from broken pottery shards (*ostraca*) or gravestone inscriptions. What was most amazing to me was Bill's ability to recall verbatim many of the passages he had read decades earlier and then apply them to a lesson or sermon.

Long before I had ever heard him talk about it, I had developed a browsing discipline of my own. My childhood home was filled with books. We had the leftovers of the libraries of both my grandfathers (both were preachers and had impressive collections). In addition, both my parents were "readers." My mother still loves to read almost anything from Shakespeare to Malcolm Muggeridge. My father, however, was the most serious reader in the house. He belonged to multiple book-buying clubs that sent a steady stream of books through the mail. He read history, as well as historical novels. He read archaeology, being especially interested in Mayan culture. Astronomy was another of his passions—one he passed on to his youngest son. Besides all these interests, there were mountains of medical journals which he methodically read and underlined, clipping articles which were specifically related to his field (cardiology).

Of all the books in our home, I remember most vividly a large leather-bound bicentennial edition of the Britannica. (The "bicentennial" in the title referred to the two hundredth year of the Britannica company, not the bicentennial of the United States!) I remember the musty smell and the fragile, thin pages with their gold edges. I remember learning to look up subjects as soon as I could make out words, and then later, as a high schooler, learning to use the massive index which took up an entire volume. Before I could read I browsed through, looking at the illustrations. To this day, much of what I know I can trace directly to that wonderful set of books. I still recognize people, places, and things I have never seen heretofore, except in those volumes.

When I was in junior high, my mother introduced me to the Harvard Classics. We had both sets: the five-foot fiction shelf and the classics set. To my dismay, not a single one of the 50 or so volumes had any pictures! I was just about to write them off when I turned to a section in one of the volumes called *Plutarch's Lives*. For some reason, long forgotten, I began to read the fascinating accounts of Plutarch. I discovered that indeed there were pictures after all—word pictures! More colorful, moving, and realistic than even the Britannica. From that day on I was hooked.

I share these stories with you to make the point that giving children the simple freedom to wade and browse through, on their own, the books in either your home or your local library can have an effect that will last a lifetime. Even before they are able to read, becoming familiar friends with books will lay the foundation for a later love affair with learning.

NINE

Some Questions About Homeschooling

O ne of the best ways to learn is to ask questions. We thought it might be helpful to include a few questions that are frequently asked by parents who are considering the homeschool lifestyle or are already teaching at home. I have attempted to answer them on the basis of my own experience and research. My answers will not be the same as everyone else's in the homeschooling movement. These are my opinions, and I am certainly not infallible. You'll need to think, pray, do some research, and then draw your own conclusions. But hopefully my insights will prove helpful!

How could I possibly be competent to teach my children?

I believe that the root of this question is fear—the fear of taking on a huge responsibility. And a huge one it is! But you can do it! You do not need to measure your God-given gifts by the world's credential-based standards. A college degree is not necessary, and it certainly does not ensure that you will make a good teacher. If you can read and write, if you have passion for your children's education, and if you are willing to make some sacrifices and work hard at it, then you have the skills and attitude that it will take. Your desire to provide the best educational experience for your children can motivate you to do just about anything.

You can rest in two things. First, that God has given you many gifts if only you will become aware of them and use them. Second, there are many curriculums available that are "new teacher" friendly, as well as having good content, practical help, graphics, and reliability. All they require is the necessary preparation that will familiarize you with what you are teaching and with the way the curriculum presents it. If you run into problems, you can usually call for help. You will find the publishers and curriculum suppliers to be the friendliest and most helpful people around. As home educators, we have the privilege to be associated with a large community of wonderful citizens—the homeschool community. Do not let yourself be dissuaded from teaching your children at home because of fear.

But the decision to homeschool does require some balance. While you can rest somewhat within your chosen curriculum, you must never underestimate what is required of you to teach. You will need to find someone to walk you through the many curriculum choices, and you need to eventually take responsibility for those choices. As a parent/teacher, you must become a good listener, an observer of your children in an arena that in the past has been abdicated to the professionals. It can be an awkward process at first, to try to articulate what you believe. It is a good idea to write out your philosophy of education and to set some clear goals. Then you can find the resources you will need to take action.

Be diligent in your efforts. Be accurate in your teaching, even if it means asking questions or looking things up in a book. By being resourceful, you teach your children to be resourceful. Don't simply lecture to your children, giving them the impression that you know everything. Participate as a learner as well! Be organized and keep good records for your children's sake. Enjoy the process. Joy is contagious!

What do you think of prepackaged curriculums?

For someone who is just starting out they are manna (food from heaven). They remove the pressure of having to make lots of decisions all at once. Most of the curriculums that I have seen are well organized and well researched, encouraging feedback from their purchasers.

Do not be surprised, however, to find that the curriculum does not provide everything that you need. One curriculum package I purchased was very good, except for the history section. I really did not like its approach. I had to research a little to find out what else was available and make a different choice for that subject area. Part of my research involved asking a few moms at one of the homeschool support group coffees. I am continually amazed by these mothers! They are informative, articulate, and strongly opinionated. They will tell you in a heartbeat what they like and why they like it. Honesty is not usually a problem in the circle of homeschool moms and dads! They speak from experience and are an invaluable resource.

After several years, I have now pieced together a very satisfying range of material that works for each of my children. We actively evaluate our progress and make minor adjustments all the time. I would recommend making a curriculum choice and working from it, rather than being overwhelmed with trying to come up with material for each subject and then giving up in frustration! When you choose a curriculum, though, the key is to not become a slave to it. The printed goals and class outlines look simple, but when you implement the lessons with your unique, creative mind, you'll find that the variables of your life situation were not included in print! Do not surrender to an attitude of defeat. Analyze the variables you are dealing with and adjust.

One of the first purchases you should make is either the *Christian Home Educators' Curriculum Manual for Elementary Grades* by Cathy Duffy or Mary Pride's *Big Book of Home Learning*. Get some advice from these experienced parents/teachers and evaluate their research for yourself. These books are informative and very well organized so that you have quick access to answers to almost any question. Review new curriculums every year to see what is available.

Although I do not limit myself to one program, I have found Sonlight curriculum to work well for many of our needs. I frequently refer to their reading lists because they are history/literature-based curriculum and one that is rich in great classic literature choices. Because Will is such an avid reader, I was glad to see they have not only a grade-level reading list, but an advanced grade-level reading list as well. In three months Will read 100 books! Many of them came from the lists provided by Sonlight.

Keep in mind that there are lots of reading lists available! You can go to the public library, find out what the public schools are reading, or check your local bookstore for ideas. Coming up with reading material will never be a problem. Your responsibility is to decide when you want your children to read different types of literature. Occasionally I want them to read some historical fiction to correlate with our history lesson. At other times they get to choose anything they want. Our main priority is to help them develop reading as an everyday habit.

What if my child has questions I can't answer, especially concerning math and science?

When it comes to math questions, I call my brother! My suggestion is to find someone in your community who is good in math. Or call a support group leader and find someone else who is using your same curriculum. But opinions will differ! Several parents had trouble using one curriculum that my brother and I loved. They found the Saxon math curriculum to be better for their needs. Find what works for you and do not be afraid to ask for help. There are now web sites that offer help and support through your home computer. Take advantage of what is available. You might want to follow the example found in *Homeschooling for Excellence* by David and Micki Colfax. Their boys were active in deciding which curriculum they wanted to use. The older boys were able to give good advice to their younger siblings. If other parents cannot answer your questions, maybe you should ask some of their children! We have found that our children are one of our best-kept secrets! They are very resourceful and love to share their experiences.

Science, for many people, can be intimidating. But you will find it is not that difficult if you study and learn the material along with your children. If you are teaching elementary grade levels, your reading comprehension will keep you well advanced as you teach.

Following a curriculum may be your best course of action in subjects you are uncomfortable with. Just remind yourself to work diligently, but never become a slave to the printed page. (If you are only looking for science material, Sonlight provides a science curriculum that can be purchased separately from the whole curriculum.)

Will homeschooled kids be able to keep up academically?

According to standardized test scores, homeschooled kids are scoring better than public school students. On this basis, homeschoolers are excelling. But such tests are not the real measure of success. Our philosophy is so very different from that of the school system. One of our parents recently compared watching for results in our children to waiting for a loaf of bread to rise. You cannot rush or quicken the process. And the most difficult aspect is that most of the rising process goes on unseen. When waiting for our children to grow and develop, we are at the mercy of how God has uniquely designed them. Trying to force the process forward only proves to be frustrating and ego-deflating for the child. Children can begin to feel as though they will never measure up. Some children who might not be ready to read until they are nine will score lower than if they were given the time to reach their full potential. When they are ready, their skills will be mastered much quicker. Research has shown that, regardless of early education, everyone equals out by the sixth grade. Our philosophy is, Why put unnecessary pressure on our children and rob them of their childhood in the process?

Many parents who had their children in public education and decided to bring them home have found that their children began learning more rapidly because the stress caused by constant comparisons with others was absent, and this allowed their children to relax and work at their own pace. The children became more resourceful and more motivated. They developed a sense of ownership in their studies, which encouraged self-governing skills (which are the hardest to teach).

Michael and I have had people in the working community—shop owners, tutors, and even college professors—say that they can see a positive difference in the children. I have always been a little skeptical because as a homeschool mom I do not want to lose an objective view. Plus I am with my children all the time and cannot always see their progress. But if being a well-rounded individual is your idea of academic success, then we certainly are a success!

But it is not just my children who have found great success in learning at home. I personally know numbers of homeschool families whose children have really excelled in the home environment. The Colfax children were even accepted into Harvard on the basis of their excellent home-school experience. Do children who receive an education at home get the kind of education that will help them develop their intellectual capacities? If you have doubts, scan this list of "homeschool graduates"!

Alexander Graham Bell
Pearl S. Buck
Charlie Chaplin
Agatha Christie
Winston Churchill
Leonardo daVinci
Charles Dickens
Thomas Edison
Jonathan Edwards
Benjamin Franklin
Robert E. Lee
Abraham Lincoln
Douglas MacArthur
Claude Monet
Wolfgang Mozart
Florence Nightingale
Franklin Delano Roosevelt
Albert Schweitzer
George Washington
John Wesley
Woodrow Wilson
Orville and Wilbur Wright

I think this list lends some support to our credibility. We do not all have to submit to what Tolstoy called the "conspiracy of dullness and futility" that some of us have found in the public system of education.

What about socialization?

One of my friends would answer this question by saying, "We try to avoid it!" Her response is humorous to those of us close to her because, though we realize the importance of "good" socialization, we think the term is getting an inordinate amount of attention. Why isn't there as much emphasis on learning to be self-governing and on individuality?

One article I read said that children needed the play, the fighting, and the working out that happens on a playground. My response is, "I have your fighting right here." The difference between the public playground and home is that our fights are well supervised and so, when a fight (verbal or physical) breaks out, we are quick to run interference and help the children learn from the experience. They are given guidelines to prevent further arguing and alternative methods to resolve future disputes.

The best way to deal with socialization is to clearly define it. According to Webster's definition, *socialize* first means "to make social; adjust to or make fit for cooperative group living." I believe we are doing a very good job of this in our own home. We are educating and equipping our children with a moral base, sound judgment, discernment, and plenty of occasions for interaction both at home and with friends and family.

The second definition is "to adapt or make conform to the common needs of a social group." First we must answer the question, What social group are we conforming to? And how much time do we want to commit to social groups? If we send our children to school, they get 30 to 40 hours a week of social group time. Then there are extracurricular group activities that occur after school. Could this perhaps be too much of a good thing? How do homeschoolers implement this aspect of socialization? Our involvement with our churches is a great example. Other social groups would include our families, friends, our organized homeschool groups and outings, co-op classes, Boy Scouts or Girl Scouts, or outside classes like ballet, gymnastics, or organized sports. These are all examples of wholesome social groups that are usually well supervised.

And is socialization always good in itself? There is good, positive socialization, and there is bad socialization. To achieve good socialization in young children there must be close supervision. The ratio between students and teachers is too great in the public school system to achieve this effectively. I have seen "good" socialization take place when Nathan is in his group session, with as little as four children to one teacher and an aide. Every altercation is addressed, and an appropriate response is given and practiced.

Another example of a good form of socialization is Mother's Day Out programs for preschoolers. Again, the ratio between teacher and children is low so the children are well supervised. These programs, which are held mostly in churches, also teach and implement good moral behavior. Character-building traits like sharing, speaking kindly, helping, and playing within a group are exercised. Once again, my children are better for having been there. This is in contrast to hearing mothers lament over their children in school. I have heard frequently, "You would not believe what they come home with!" I have yet to hear an argument that can convince me that unsupervised socialization is better than being at home.

The last definition of *socialization* is "to subject to governmental ownership and control; nationalize." No thank you. We have lost too many lives for the sake of freedom of individuality to make ourselves slaves to government protocol. If our government officials would look and listen, they would see rising a great movement that will produce some of the best citizens this country has seen in a long while.

How many hours a day does it require? How much preparation?

The time required depends on the ages of your children and the educational material you have chosen. The older the children get, the more time it takes. In a couple of years, they will take even more initiative in their lessons, much like a college student, and I will not have to walk them through so many "tools" of the trade.

On the average now, it takes three to five hours a week for me to review work, keep records, and plan for the next week. But we view learning as an all-day exercise, so generally speaking, from the moment they get up until the time they are asleep, they are learning. But if you want to know how many hours we spend with books, it averages out to about four a day. We homeschool all year, taking breaks that we have organized into our personal calendar. There are many different combinations you can use to reach the average 36-week study course. Out of 52 weeks, you have 16 weeks to be creative with. You can school for nine weeks on and four weeks off the entire year, or you may want to school all year, taking three weeks off at Easter and Christmas, and ten weeks during the summer. Another option is to school only four days a week and adjust by days. You will enjoy your "vacation" time so much more if you allot the time in advance.

How do you teach children who are at different grade levels at the same time?

What we have done has been to coordinate as many subjects as we can. The schedule for the day remains the same for both children, even though the books may be age-appropriate. Language arts, math, and reading are subjects that require age-appropriate material. So while Katie works through a third-grade level of spelling, Will works on a workbook that fits his own level. But there are other subjects that we can all work on together. Subjects such as Bible, character-building stories, science, history, geography, Latin, and read-aloud literature are all done together, which saves a great deal of time and energy. Since Katie and Will are only one grade level apart, this isn't too difficult. But there are many families where the gap is much greater, and they still find it possible to combine subjects.

We enjoy our times of learning together. Our read-aloud time often finds Maggie curled up in my lap. We are currently reading *The Wind in the Willows* by Kenneth Grahame. Maggie loves to hear more about the rat and mole, though she is only three! Nathan likes the silly toad the best. Though not officially schooling yet, they join us because of the warm atmosphere and because it delays their bedtime!

Segregation by grade level is not necessary for every subject, especially if you want the older children to be involved with the younger. It helps the children to move ahead, having the freedom to do as much extra as they can and want to do.

What if my friends and family are opposed?

You just need to realize that sometimes people will misunderstand. You are part of a pioneering movement that people have trouble adjusting to. We are no longer part of the "norm," and some people are threatened by your willingness to "go against the flow." My advice is to not become defensive or try to argue with them. Let the qualities they see developing in your children be your answer. Your children will be a living testimony to the success of the homeschool movement.

Surround yourself with kindred spirits, those bosom buddies who understand the challenges and delights of homeschooling. Find a support group and fill your tank with encouragement, discussions, acknowledgments of problems and their solutions, and just the simple fun of being with others (see, we are social after all!). Do not try to convince anyone who does not see the value of what you are doing, unless they are open-minded and want to hear more. We are called to set ourselves apart. Not everyone will understand.

Is homeschooling legal?

Homeschooling is now legal in all states, but each state has different requirements. You can register under the public school system or under the umbrella of a private school (which is the route we took). For any legal information, contact the Homeschool Legal Defense Association (HSLDA). HSLDA also provides books and an educational course through the internet. They are a valuable resource and publish the *Home School Court Report*, a bimonthly publication that keeps us informed on current litigation proceedings and other informative topics (see resource list in back of book).

Where do I get materials?

Here is a list of a few suppliers:

Barnabus Books
Elgin, IL 60120
708-741-8999
(Carole Joy Seid: hard-to-find classical and
Christian literature)

Beautiful Feet Books
139 Main St.
Sandwich, MA 02563
508-833-8626
(Russ and Rea Berg: history through literature)

Canadian Home Education Resources
7 Stanley Crescent S.W.
Calgary, Alberta T2S 1G1
Canada

Christian Liberty Press
502 W. Euclid Ave.
Arlington Heights, IL 60004

Cuisenaire Co. of America, Inc.
Materials for Learning Mathematics and Science
P.O. Box 5026
White Plains, NY 10602-5026

great

Elijah Company
Route 2, Box 100B
Crossville, TN 38555
615-456-6284

Farm Country General Store
Route 2, Box 412
Metamora, IL 61548
800-551-FARM

great

God's World Publications (God's World Magazines)
P.O. Box 2330
Asheville, NC 28802-2330
800-951-5437

good bargain prices but you have to order early

Great Christian Books
P.O. Box 8000
229 South Bridge St.
Elkton, MD 21922
800-775-5422
(An extensive free catalog)

Green Pastures Press
7102 Lynn Rd. NE
Minerva, OH 44657
330-895-3291

Greenleaf Press
1570 Old LaGuardo Road
Lebanon, TN 37087
615-449-1617
(Rob and Cyndy Shearer)

Hearthside Homeschool Helps
74 Lynn Dr.
Woodbury, NJ 08096
609-845-3681
(Specializing in KONOS materials)

good

Lifetime Books and Gifts
3900 Chalet Suzanne Dr.
Lake Wales, FL 33853-7763

National Wildlife Federation
8925 Leesburg Pike
Vienna, VA 22184-0001

Rod and Staff Publishers, Inc.
P.O. Box 3, Hwy 172
Crockett, KY 41413-0003
606-522-4348

Ruark's Home and School Accessories
8232 N. County Road 150 East
Pittsboro, IN 46167-9466
317-892-4791

Sonlight Curriculum
8121 South Grant Way
Littleton, CO 80122
303-730-6292

Sycamore Tree Center for Home Education
2179 Meyer Place
Costa Mesa, CA 92627
714-650-4466

Timberdoodle Company
E. 1510 Spencer Lake Rd.
Shelton, WA 98584
206-426-0672

Usborne Books
P.O. Box 470663
Tulsa, OK 74147-0663

Whole Heart Catalog
P.O. Box 228
Walnut Springs, TX 76690
817-797-2142

Recommended Resources

I wrote this book from a personal, heartfelt point of view, and that is reflected in this list of personal favorites. This list will provide some very practical resources that you can use in your own homeschool journey. These are books which have educated, inspired, and challenged us. I hope you find them to be helpful.

Curriculum Resource Manuals

Cathy Duffy. *The Christian Home Educator's Curriculum Manual.*

> This is an excellent resource. Cathy interacts with the products, giving insightful suggestions concerning learning styles. She deals with nearly every topic a homeschooling family would want to read about. Volume I covers elementary and preschool. Volume II focuses on junior and senior high.

Edward Bernard Fry, Ph.D., Jacqueline E. Kress, Ed.D., and Dona Lee Fountoukidis, Ed.D. *The Reading Teacher's Book of Lists*, 3d ed. Prentice Hall.

> This reference tool is one to keep near your desk at all times. It is, very simply, a book which lists the rules and word usages that you may have forgotten long ago. Now you won't have to search for answers to basic questions since they are compiled in this one book.

Mary Pride. *The Big Book of Home Learning.*
Crossway Books.

> There are four volumes to this comprehensive listing of every curriculum, product, philosophy, magazine, organization and catalog. Mary's reviews are opinionated and enlightening. Volume 1, Getting Started; volume 2, Preschool and Elementary; volume 3, High School; volume 4 includes music, art, and afterschool activities. A great resource!

The Philosophy and Practice of Homeschooling

Vicki A. Brady. *The Basic Steps to Successful Homeschooling.* Vital Issues Press.

> Don't be fooled by the word "basic"! These seemingly simple steps can make or break your efforts. Vicki gives step-by-step instructions on all the practicalities of homeschooling—the kind of insights that come only from experience. The chapter I have returned to over and over again is on home skills. As basic as that may seem, that's where I found the help I needed.

David and Micki Colfax. *Homeschooling for Excellence.* Warner Books.

> A real-life story of a family that chose to live a more isolated lifestyle and teach their children at home. This is a success story in that three of their four sons (the fourth wasn't old enough for college when the book was published) all went on to Harvard. While Harvard may not be your goal, their family story can lend some academic credibility to those searching for it. It is an inspiring, informative book.

Cathy Duffy. *Government Nannies.* Noble Publishing Associates

> Cathy provides us with facts and cases that reveal the direction our government is headed with "Outcome-Based Education" and "Goals 2000." The information is alarming and important.

John Taylor Gatto. *Dumbing Us Down*. New Society Publishers.

> Look inside the public schoolroom through the eyes of a teacher and see all that you can see! Mr. Gatto's tactful, insightful conclusions about the state of public education today serve to strengthen our decision to be different! You may find yourself, as I did, being able to find examples from your own life for every one of his points. Scary!

Terry W. Glaspey. *Children of a Greater God*. Harvest House Publishers.

> After reading so many books on practical issues, I was finally able to indulge myself in the issues of the heart. Terry adds a wonderful depth and dimension to the rigorous and demanding lifestyle of homeschooling. This book also includes a list for building your classical musical library and a great list of suggested children's books. With references and quotes throughout, this book will add color to your commitment. Highly recommended!

E. D. Hirsch. *Books to Build On*. Bantam Doubleday Dell Publishing Group, Inc.

> A handy reference for those putting together a curriculum and needing suggestions for reading. Books are broken down by grade level.

___. *Cultural Literacy*. Vintage Books/Random House.

> I purchased this book for myself years ago because I was constantly coming up against words and terms I didn't understand. I so appreciate Mr. Hirsch identifying a nationwide epidemic and dealing with it.

___. *A First Dictionary of Cultural Literacy*. Houghton Mifflin Company.

> This edition is similar to the first except it is designed especially for children. Great resource.

___. *What Your 1st Grader Needs to Know*. Bantam Doubleday Dell Publishing Group, Inc.

> The Core Knowledge Series, of which this is the first, covers by grade level what your child should know. These guidebooks are very useful and perfect for those of us who like to make sure we are covering all the bases.

Homeschooling Today. Magazine.

> This is a valuable tool for any homeschooling family to read. It has feature articles about almost every issue you can think of. It also has helpful lesson starters on history, art, literature, science and music. Their reviews will keep you abreast of the latest resources. My favorite section is "Understanding the Arts," and there is always a beautiful painting in the center and a lesson on the artist. This magazine is published six times a year.

> Homeschooling Today
> 6011 Rodman St.
> Suite 301
> Hollywood, FL 33023
> Ph. 954/962-1930

Diane Lopez. *Teaching Children*. Crossway Books.

> This is where your education as a parent/teacher begins. Diane teaches you how to avoid being locked into prepackaged curriculums. She walks you through each subject and each grade level through sixth grade in a very thorough way. If you have questions on Charlotte Mason's methods, like "narration" or "living books," you will find answers here. The introduction is written by Susan Schaeffer Macaulay.

Susan Schaeffer Macaulay. *For the Children's Sake*. Crossway Books.

> A very practical approach to education from a Christian perspective. This book was a turning point for me. Susan introduces us to Charlotte Mason, her perspective on teaching children and her unique insights. A must!

Raymond and Dorothy Moore. *Better Late Than Early.*
Reader's Digest Press.

This book offers information from the Moore's research to
support delayed schooling—waiting until your child is
ready to begin schooling. This is a source that will help
you relax and not burden your child with unnecessary
expecations.

___. *Home-Built Discipline.* Thomas Nelson Publishers.

Good practical applications for character building. The
Moores cover the different developmental stages and possible problems, along with solutions. As always, they provide real-life examples. They present discipline as being
creative and positive, rather than negative.

___. *Home-Grown Kids.* Word Books.

A thorough look at the developmental stages from birth to
nine years of age. The text is colored with real-life situations to support their points. The Moores cover topics that
relate to the heart and mind. This book provides a good,
basic understanding of children.

___. *Home-Spun Schools.* Word Books.

Here is a collection of stories from a wide variety of people. If you need encouragement when homeschooling
seems impossible, read a few of these inspirational stories
to prime your pump.

___. *Minding Your Own Business.* Thomas Nelson
Publishers.

Practical advice on home management. The Moores offer
a vast selection of possible cottage industries and their advantages and disadvantages. They show the necessity of a
conscientious awareness of avoiding wastefulness and
demonstrate how to teach financial responsibility to your
children.

___. *Successful Homeschool Family Handbook*. Thomas
Nelson Publishers.

> This book seems to cover it all. It provides encouragement
> to those who doubt, practical steps and how to's, several
> stories from other homeschooling parents and their
> unique situations, advice on college, a history of the home-
> school movement, and the "Moore formula." All of this
> wisdom from the "grandparents" of teaching at home. A
> great resource.

Mary Pride. *School Proof*. Crossway Books.

> This book offers a witty, "get to the point" approach to ed-
> ucation. Mary covers a wide range of topics that are prac-
> tical for teaching at home and gives good reasons for
> breaking educational rules, and her practical nature will
> have you laughing out loud. If you are looking for
> strength in your resolve, you might start here.

Edith Schaeffer. *The Hidden Art of Homemaking*. Tyndale
House Publishers.

> A very inspiring and encouraging book on enjoying our
> creative gifts. She covers many different creative outlets
> to practice within your home and gives us permission to
> play! Give yourself a treat that will benefit you for years
> to come.

Douglas Wilson. *Recovering the Lost Tools of Learning*.
Crossway Books.

> This book is full of great material on Christian education.
> Mr. Wilson opens your eyes to the present crisis of our na-
> tion's educational system. He looks briefly at home-
> schooling, but advocates the "classical education." For
> those not wanting to homeschool, this is an alternative.
> You need to give this book a good look—even if you dis-
> agree with some of its conclusions.

Helpful Book Lists

Terry Glaspey. *Great Books of the Christian Tradition.*
Harvest House Publishers.

> This is a great resource. The book lists included here are organized according to time periods, which can really be an advantage when you need supplemental reading material or want to expose your children to the writers of a particular era. This is a great book to keep on hand for reference. It includes a complete index of the authors that are discussed.

William Kilpatrick and Gregory and Suzanne M. Wolfe.
Books That Build Character. Simon and Schuster Publishers.

> The entries in this book are arranged by category and age level. The books were selected for their ability to communicate moral values.

Bible Resources

The Golden Children's Bible.
Western Publishing Company.

> Lots of wonderful illustrations with a shortened text to help young minds not get distracted.

The Holy Bible, New International Version.
Zondervan Publishing House.

> This is the translation of Scripture we use. In class, the children use the Ultrathin Reference Edition because it is easy for them to handle. We also keep a reference Bible handy for deeper study.

Selina Hastings, illustrated by M. Eric Thomas.
The Children's Illustrated Bible. Star Song.

> Very effective teaching tool. This was our Bible curriculum for an entire year. We explored geography through the multiplicity of maps and learned about foods, clothing, and historical artifacts. This book is a must!

Karyn Henley, illustrated by W. Dennas Davis.
The Beginner's Bible. Zondervan Publishers.

> This was an effective reader for the children when they
> were first learning to read for themselves. The stories
> are nice and short, and the colorful illustrations kept
> the children's attention. Recommended for younger
> children.

Calvin Miller. *The Book of Jesus.* Simon and Schuster
Publishers.

> A comprehensive collection of writings about Jesus. From
> lyric, to poetry, to prophetic narrative, to prose, to testi-
> monies, you will delight in the broad array of voices that
> Calvin has compiled for us to "hear." Older children
> through adults. Wonderful!

Eugene Peterson. *The Message.* NavPress.

> A contemporary rendition of Scripture using everyday
> language. This translation adds a fresh perspective to
> reading Scripture. I recommend this for older elementary
> children through adults. The different books available:
> The Old Testament Wisdom Books, the New Testament,
> Psalms, Proverbs, and Job.

L. J. Sattgast, illustrated by Russ Flint. *My Very First Bible.*
Harvest House Publishers.

> This is my all-time favorite Bible storybook for
> preschoolers. The length of the stories is just right and
> the illustrations are so lively and dramatic they make
> the stories come alive. This book is a must for younger
> children!

Catherine F. Vos. *The Child's Story Bible.* Eerdmans.

Character-Building Books

Christine Allison. *Teach Your Children Well.*
Delacorte Press.

A collection of short stories, poems, and fables with traditional values.

William Bennett. *The Book of Virtue*s and *The Moral Com-*
pass. Simon and Schuster.

Got + μ.μ.

These books are great for getting into the habit of reading together. Both comprehensive collections provide enjoyment for all age groups. That is why they are great for the family setting. Plus, most of the stories are short. Highly recommended.

___. Illustrated by Michael Hague. *The Children's Book of Virtues.*

The stories come to life with Michael's brilliant illustrations. A wonderful read-aloud for children.

Michael Card. *Close Your Eyes So You Can See.* Harvest House Publishers.

Michael wrote this collection of fictional stories around the children mentioned in the Bible during Jesus' life. The blend of historical accuracy, perspective, and beautiful illustrations by Stephen Marchesi make a great book for devotional readings. (Of course, I like it!)

Ron and Rebekah Coriell. *A Child's Book of Character Building*, Books 1 and 2. Fleming H. Revell.

These books provide short explanations for character traits in the context of home, school, and play. Each trait has a Bible verse and story to support it, and then it is translated into what it looks like in action. Very helpful.

Hannah Hurnard, arranged by Dian Layton, illustrated by JoAnn Edington. *Hind's Feet on High Places.* Destiny Image Publishers.

This retelling of the classic is suitable for children. A wonderful allegory and a must for building character.

Mildred A. Martin. Green Pastures Press.

Storytime with the Millers (ages 4–8)
Prudence and the Millers (ages 7–14)
Schooldays and the Millers (ages 7–14)
Wisdom and the Millers [Proverbs] (ages 6–13)
Missionary Stories with the Millers (all ages)

These are wonderful stories that capture the heart of Scripture. The context is in the home of an Amish family. These stories are warm, challenging, and applicable. They offer powerful images of what godly character "looks" like. Highly recommended!

Emile Poulsson. *Lessons from the Farmyard.* Christian Liberty Press.

We travel to the farmyard and read about a mischievous little rabbit as he learns an important lesson. Just plain fun! Recommended for younger children.

Handwriting

Getty and Dubay. *Italic Handwriting Series.* Continuing Education Press.

This handwriting series involves learning only one letter for both manuscript and cursive. The children learn to use joiners in between the letters when they transition to cursive writing. This is our son Will's favorite.

Retzer and Hoshina. *A Reason for Writing.* A Concerned Communications Publication.

Done

This is our daughter Katie's choice for handwriting. She likes the precision of cursive letters; for her it is more creative. We also like the fact that the practice words are biblical. At the end of the lesson there is a complete Bible verse to be written on the border pages in the back of the workbook.

Language Arts

ACSI Spelling. Association of Christian Schools International.

Good

We have had success with these books. Each lesson has a variety of exercises that help students learn their spelling words. They also include a glossary in the back of the book for easy access. This is the best I have seen yet. Highly recommended.

Christian Liberty Nature Reader. Christian Liberty Press.

Good

A delightful set of readers that focus on nature. Instead of presenting fictional reading, they are instilling what is true and foundational to the world of our children.

Pathway Readers. Pathway Publishers.

An early reader series that we particularly liked. Probably because it had to do with farm life!

Samuel L. Blumenfeld. *Alphaphonics.* The Paradigm Company.

Katie and Will both learned to read through this book. It is a primer for beginning readers that uses phonics instruction. A teacher's manual in the back refers to each lesson as you teach. Highly recommended.

O.K.

Hall and Price. *Explode the Code*, Primers and Books 1–8.
Educators Publishing Service, Inc.

> Katie and Will both enjoy the Explode the Code series.
> They protested when I considered changing! Beginning
> with basic letter recognition and usage, they cover a wide
> range of letter sounds, consonants, vowels, consonant
> blends, three-letter consonant blends, and so on with tests
> in the back of each book.

Mary F. Hyde. *English for the Thoughtful Child*.
Greenleaf Press.

Good

> A good first course for English. The lessons integrate real
> life with simple, thoughtful approaches to the writing pro-
> cess. It also stresses grammar and composition. We have
> thoroughly enjoyed working through this text.

Strayer and Simpson. *Learning Language Arts Through
Literature*. Common Sense Press.

> This is a great package of material. Each grade level (first
> grade–high school) has a literature-based approach to lan-
> guage. There is a teacher's manual and a student activity
> book color-coded according to grade level. Easy to use
> with comprehensive exercises. Highly recommended.

Mathematics

Miquon. Key Curriculum Press.

Has holes

> Six levels of math are taught with this curriculum. You
> will need the Lab Sheet Annotations as a teaching aid and
> cuissenaire rods for the math manipulatives. We like this
> curriculum and have had good success with it. But you
> must understand the process because it has an unorthodox
> way of teaching.

Larson. *Saxon Math*. Saxon Publishers, Inc.

> After Miquon, all of our children transitioned to Saxon. With Saxon's new third-grade-level course, you can switch earlier if you choose. This curriculum covers practical usages of math, rulers, thermometers, clocks, flash cards, number patterns, and coins. Time-consuming lessons, but well worth it.

Social Studies
(History, Geography, Cultural Studies)

To even begin to offer an adequate list of social studies resources would take forever. At this point I suggest you order the *Greenleaf Press Curriculum Guide*, *Beautiful Feet Curriculum Guide*, and *Sonlight Curriculum Guide*. You can also look through the curriculum manuals for a comprehensive list of what is available.

Biographies are wonderful for putting children in touch with real people. Anne Morrow Lindbergh's writings taught me more than most history textbooks because she writes about real people and real adventures. By looking through the window of individuals we can learn a great deal.

Just for fun, here are some of our favorites.

Factbook of History. Mimosa Books, Random House.

Usborne Book of World History. Usborne.

American Girls Series. Pleasant Hill Company:
> *Felicity* series (1700s)
> *Kirsten* series (1800s)
> *Addy* series (1864)
> *Samantha* series (1904)
> *Molly* series (1944)

> Pleasant Hill Company also has a history curriculum that compares education between different time periods. They can be contacted at: Pleasant Company, 8400 Fairway Place, P.O. Box 620190, Middleton, WI 53562-0190, 1-800-845-0005.

T. L. Tedrow. *The Days of Laura Ingalls Wilder*. Thomas Nelson Publishers.

> Follow a pioneering family West. Great reading as a history supplement. Both fun and sober adventures are woven into the fabric of one family's life to give a healthy dose of reality.

D'Aulaire Series

> *Leif the Lucky* (Beautiful Feet Books)
>
> *Columbus* (Doubleday)
>
> *Pocahontas* (Doubleday)
>
> *George Washington* (Doubleday)
>
> *Benjamin Franklin* (Doubleday)
>
> *Abraham Lincoln* (Doubleday)
>
> *D'Aulares' Book of Greek Myths* (Doubleday)

> The D'Aulares' books are all great to have. They are large and colorfully illustrated. The text is informative and full of adventure.

Leaders in Action Series (Highland Books)

> Terry W. Glaspey. *Not a Tame Lion: The Spiritual Legacy of C.S. Lewis.*

> George Grant. *Carry a Big Stick: The Uncommon Heroism of Theodore Roosevelt.*

> Stephen Mansfield. *Never Give In: The Extraordinary Character of Winston Churchill.*

> David Vaughn. *Give Me Liberty: The Christian Patriotism of Patrick Henry.*

> J. Stephen Wilkins. *Call of Duty: The Sterling Nobility of Robert E. Lee.*

> The Leader in Action Series is fascinating reading for older children or adults. Michael and I have learned a great deal from this insightful series.

George Grant. *Patriot's Handbook.* Cumberland House, Inc.

> Mr. Grant reminds us of our heritage by combining poems, speeches, quotes, songs, and profiles from American presidents and other key leaders. Reading level: high school to adult.

Holling Clancy Holling. Houghton Mifflin Company.

> *Paddle-to-the-Sea* (Caldecott Honor Book)
> Follow a carved canoe from Lake Superior to the Atlantic Ocean.
>
> *Tree in the Trail*
> A cottonwood tree is our spy, revealing the secrets of over two hundred years of the Santa Fe Trail.
>
> *Seabird* (Newberry Honor Book)
> Follow four generations of seafarers aboard a whaler, a clipper ship, a steamer, and an airplane.
>
> *Minn of the Mississippi* (Newberry Honor Book)
> Travel with Minn, a turtle, from the source of the Mississippi through America's heartland to the Gulf of Mexico.
>
> History and geography are woven within the context of stories. These books are large and wonderfully illustrated.

Usborne Book of World Geography. Usborne.

Eyewitness Books. Alfred A. Knopf.

America's Providential History. Mark A. Beliles and Stephen X
K. McDowell. Providence Foundation.   Got '

> This is a story of the history of America from a Christian perspective. One of our foundational text books.

God's World Publications
> *God's Big World*
> *Sharing God's World*
> *Exploring God's World*

Weekly news publications for children from a Christian perspective. This tool keeps us informed on current events.

God's World Publications
P.O. Box 2330
Asheville, NC 28805
704-253-8063

Children Around the World series. Eerdmans.

Antoine and the Magic Coin
Carlos the Street Boy Who Found a Home
Cayna the Girl No One Wanted
Chebet and the Lost Goat
Dawa Bema the Uncertain Monk
Nikolai the Boy Who Ran Away
Sandy the Girl Who was Rescued

National Geographic. National Geographic Society.

Monthly journal. A great resource to keep within reach.

National Geographic Society
17th and M Sts. N.W.
Washington, D.C. 20036

Science and Nature

The Audubon Society Field Guides. Knopf.
North American Reptiles and Amphibians
North American Mammals
North American Insects and Spiders
North American Wildflowers

These books are great for packing around. The cover is durable, and the photographs are brilliant. A must for your library. (Keep in children's reach!).

Usborne Science Books.

The Usborne First Guide to the Universe
The Usborne Living World Encyclopedia
The Usborne Book of Knowledge

The Usborne Science Activities, vols. 1 and 2
The Usborne Science Encyclopedia
Usborne Mysteries and Marvels of Nature

Usborne is known for its busy, fact-filled pages. These books are great to follow step-by-step or just to dabble in and out of. (Another source to keep within children's reach.)

Janice VanCleave. John Wiley and Sons, Inc.

✓ *Biology for Every Kid*
✓ *Chemistry for Every Kid*
✓ *Earth Science for Every Kid*
Physics for Every Kid

For those who are timid—Janice does a friendly treatment of these subjects. Very practical and applicable lessons. She provides a list of materials, step-by-step instructions, and illustrations. Janice always makes science fun!

National Wildlife Federation monthly magazines

Great

Your Big Backyard
Ranger Rick

These magazines are filled with great photographs. The images are large and clear. Our children are delighted when they open the mailbox and quick to read the information as soon as the magazines arrive. Great resource for science and nature studies.

Learning Styles

Cynthia Tobias. Focus on the Family Publishing.

✓ *The Way They Learn*
Every Child Can Succeed

Learn how to observe your children in the context of learning styles. Cynthia does a fine job of illustrating differences in personalities.

Fine Arts/Music

Rembrandt and the Bible. Magna Books.

> This is a collection of illustrated stories from the Old and New Testaments in the form of paintings, etchings, and drawings. It is a wonderful browsing resource. We have used this book during Bible lessons to see how Rembrandt interpreted visually the stories we are reading. This book serves as an example of how art can be used to clarify, enhance, and glorify the Lord in the process. Biblical text included with explanatory notes by Hidde Hoekstra. ISBN 1-85422-1469.

Rien Poortvliet. *Noah's Ark.* Abrams.

> This book is fabulous. Rien does not show simpy finished paintings but includes drawings in stages. This is what children need to be exposed to the "process" of art. One page, for example, is of a lion in many different positions. Rien has little commentary notes on the pages in his own handwriting and sometimes splotches of watercolor that make you wonder if his brush was dripping. The artwork is "living"! A must!

The Usborne Story of Painting (Usborne)

Marie Hablitzel and Kim Stitzer. *A Drawing and Handwriting Course.*

Lucy Micklethwait. *A Child's Book of Art.* Dorling Kindersley.

Jude Welton. *Tate Gallery Drawing.* Dorling Kindersley.

Draw-Write-Now series. Barker Creek Publishing

> Book 1: On the Farm, Kids and Critters, Storybook Characters
>
> Book 2: Christopher Columbus, Harvest Time, Weather
>
> Book 3: North America, Native Americans, Pilgrims
>
> Book 4: The Cold Lands, Eskimos, Animals of the Polar Region

Book 5: The United States, Abraham Lincoln, George Washington

Book 6: On the Land, Life in Ponds and Rivers, In the Sea

Book 7: Animals of the World, Part 1

Book 8: Animals of the World, Part 2

Neil Ardley with Music by Paul Ruders. *A Young Person's Guide to Music*. Dorling Kindersley.

This book comes with an accompanying CD. It is divided into two parts: how music is made and the history of music. Wonderful graphics. The recordings were made in association with the BBC Symphony Orchestra.

The Usborne First Book of Music. Usborne.

A comprehensive glance at music. A good resource to keep within your child's reach.

Milton Cross and David Ewen. *The Milton Cross New Encyclopedia of the Great Composers and Their Music*. Doubleday.

Patrick Kavanaugh. *Raising Musical Kids*. Vine Books.

This is a practical and yet thorough approach to introducing your children to great music.

Classical Kids (audio tape series).

"Mr. Bach Comes to Call"
"Beethoven Lives Upstairs"
"Mozart's Magic Fantasy"
"Vivaldi's Ring of Mystery"
"Tchaikovsky Discovers America"

A dramatic presentation of the lives of these great composers, with samples of their musical legacies woven in. We have found these to be very entertaining.

Michael Card. *Sleep Sound in Jesus*. Harvest House Publishing.

> This book accompanies the recording of lullabies with the same title (Sparrow Records). The book includes each song, along with a devotional section written by Michael.

Michael Card. *Come to the Cradle*. Sparrow Records.

> This is another collection of lullabies recorded by Michael with Christine Dente adding vocals. The accompanying book is no longer in print.

Some Personal Favorites

Because there are so many lists and choices available, we thought we would each share our top ten favorite books.

Maggie (age 3) and Nathan (age 4)

> Judi and Ron Barrett. *Cloudy with a Chance of Meatballs.*
> Jan Brett. *The Mitten.*
> ✓ Margaret Wise Brown. *Goodnight Moon.*
> ___. *The Runaway Bunny.*
> Jane Dyer, illustrator. *The Random Book of Bedtime Stories.*
> ✓ P. D. Eastman. *Are You My Mother?*
> Mem Fox. *Hattie and the Fox.*
> Richard Scarry. *Richard Scarry's Best First Book Ever.* Random House.
> ✓ Dr. Seuss. *Green Eggs and Ham.*
> Esphyr Slobodkina. *Caps for Sale.*

Will (age 8)

> Lynne Reid Banks. *The Indian in the Cupboard* (trilogy).
> John Cunliffe. *John Cunliffe's Dragon Stories.* Hippo.
> Ruth Styles Gannett. *My Father's Dragon* (trilogy).
> Kenneth Grahame. *The Wind in the Willows.*
> ___. Michael Hague, illustrator. *The Reluctant Dragon.*
> Homer. *The Odyssey.* Wishbone Classic retold by Joanne Mattern.
> ✓ C. S. Lewis. *The Lion, the Witch, and the Wardrobe.*

Edward Marshall. *Three by the Sea.*
James Marshall. *Fox on the Job.*
Bill Waterson. *Calvin & Hobbes.* (Just about all of them!)

Katie (age 10)

Amazing Otters. National Geographic Society.
The Bible.
Serendipity reader series.
Joy Adamson. *Born Free.*
✓Louisa May Alcott. *Little Women.*
Kenneth Grahame. *The Wind in the Willows.*
✓James Herriott. *James Herriott's Treasury for Children.*
R. D. Lawrence. *Wolves.* Sierra Club Wildlife Library.
Lois Lenski. *Strawberry Girl.*
✓E. B. White. *Charlotte's Web.*

Susan (age 20+)

Jane Austen. *Pride and Prejudice.*
Charlotte Bronte. *Jane Eyre.*
Wilkie Collins. *The Woman in White.*
Charles Dickens. *A Tale of Two Cities.*
F. M. Dostoevsky. *The Brothers Karamozov.*
Victor Hugo. *Les Miserables.*
C. S. Lewis. The Narnia Series.
Anne Morrow Lindbergh. *Gift from the Sea.*
___. *War Within and Without.*
Edith Wharton. *Ethan Frome.*

I also recommend for fun:

The Chrysostom Society. *The Classics We've Read, the Difference They've Made.* McCracken Press.

> Eighteen well-known Christian writers interact with their favorite authors and tell why they like them.

Michael (age 20+). I thought it would be a treat to have the books he's listed on his website.

Here is a partial and growing list of the books which have influenced my thoughts about God and my faith in Jesus Christ. Reading other people's work, their thoughts, the truth they have found in Jesus is an important part of seeking God. If you should read any of these books I recommend, I pray that you will be encouraged and that the Spirit of God will lead you into truth.
—Michael Card

Wendell Berry. *Openings* (favorite poetry), *The Hidden Wound* (thoughtful look at slavery), *The Wild Birds* (contains some of the best short stories in American literature). Harold Best. *Music Through the Eyes of Faith.*

F. F. Bruce. *New Testament History.*

Deitrich Bonhoeffer. *Cost of Discipleship* (radically changed my life), *Christ the Center. Life Together* (a wonderful blueprint for community).

Frederick Buechner. Almost anything by Buechner is excellent. Some of his books that have impacted me most are *Godric* (a novel about a saint who doesn't want to be a saint), *The Faces of Jesus* (a coffee-table book of art from the life of Jesus), *Telling the Truth, Magnificent Defeat, Hungering Dark, Sacred Journey, Now and Then, Telling Secrets* (autobiographical, wonderful!), and *Son of Laughter.*

Robert Cahill. *How the Irish Saved Civilization.*

Alfred Edersheim. *Life and Times of Jesus the Messiah* (best background to the New Testament).

Ken Gire. *Windows of the Soul.* (Susan recommends everyone treat themselves to this contemporary author and especially this book.)

Abraham Heschel. *God's Search for Man* (absolute best book on prayer), *The Prophets* (absolute best book on prophets), *I Asked for Wonder* (an overview of his thoughts).

William Lane. *Mark* (NIC), *Hebrews* (Word).

Brennan Manning. *Lion and Lamb: The Relentless Tenderness of Jesus* (possibly the best devotional book written in our time!), *Signature of Jesus.*

Mike Mason. *The Mystery of Marriage* (best book on marriage).

Henri Nouwen. *Compassion, The Genesee Diary, In the Name of Jesus, Beyond the Mirror.*

Calvin Miller. *Singer Trilogy, Valiant Papers, Book of Jesus.*

Malcom Muggeridge. *Jesus Rediscovered; Jesus, the Man Who Lives.*

Eugene Peterson. *Reversed Thunder* (best book on Revelation).

Chet Raymo. *The Soul of the Night* (personal favorite on astronomy).

Oliver Sacks (writes with more compassion than anyone I know). *The Man Who Mistook His Wife for a Hat, Awakenings, Seeing Voices.*

Calvin Seerveld. *Rainbows for a Fallen World* (the book on aesthetics and faith).

These are some favorites. I left out C. S. Lewis and some others whom I guess everyone reads. Some other favorites are Dumas (especially *The Count of Monte Cristo*), *Dear Theo: Letters of Vincent van Gogh*, almost anything by Flannery O'Connor, Hugo, T. H. White, Robert Coles. I am surely leaving some biggies out, but these are the ones that come immediately to mind.

Scripture Passages Illustrated
by Michael Card Songs

One of the things that people often say to me when they talk about Michael's music is how much his songs have helped to open up their understanding of the Scriptures. Most of his songs illustrate passages or narratives from the biblical text. His imaginative insights into these stories can be a great help in making the biblical truths a part of one's life.

Because so many homeschoolers make Bible study a part of their education, I thought it might be helpful to make a list of the songs with the passages they refer to. That way, they can be used as a supplementary resource with your children. When you study a passage, you might listen to the corresponding song. I think that your children will find the inclusion of the songs to be both fun and spiritually enriching.

I have listed the Scripture passage in the first column, the song title in the second, and the CD/cassette on which the song can be found in the third.

The Old Testament

Scripture Reference	Song Title	Album
Genesis 1–3	The Beginning	The Beginning
Genesis 17:1-8	El Shaddai	The Early Works
Genesis 21	They Called Him Laughter	The Beginning
Genesis 22	God Will Provide a Lamb	The Beginning
Genesis 28; 32	Asleep on Holy Ground	The Beginning
Genesis 28:10ff	Dreaming Jacob's Dream	Sleep Sound in Jesus
Exodus	In the Wilderness	The Beginning
Exodus 34:29ff	A Face That Shone	The Beginning
Leviticus 25	Jubilee	The Beginning
Numbers 6:24	Barocha	The Beginning
Numbers 24:4-9	Lift Up the Suffering Symbol	The Beginning
Deuteronomy 6	Meditation #3, Shema	The Beginning
Deuteronomy 30:4	The Word Is So Near	The Beginning
2 Chronicles 7:14	Heal Our Land	Joy in the Journey
Job	Job Suite	The Way of Wisdom
Psalm 13	How Long?	The Way of Wisdom
Psalms 22; 69	The Death of a Son	The Way of Wisdom
Psalm 23	My Shepherd	The Way of Wisdom
Psalm 95	Come and Worship the Lord	Brother to Brother
Psalm 121	My Help	The Way of Wisdom
Psalm 139	Search Me and Know Me	The Way of Wisdom
Psalm 139:11ff	Even the Darkness Is Light to Him	Sleep Sound in Jesus
Proverbs	The Way of Wisdom	The Way of Wisdom
Ecclesiastes	Under the Sun	The Way of Wisdom
Song of Solomon	Arise My Love	The Way of Wisdom
The Prophets	The Prophet	The Word
	Then They Will Know	The Word
	The Kingdom	The Word
Isaiah 6:11	And a Little Child Shall Lead	The Word
Isaiah 7:14	The Promise	The Promise/The Final Word
Isaiah 7:14	Immanuel	The Final Word
Isaiah 8:14	Scandalon	Scandalon
Isaiah 9:6ff	Unto Us a Son Is Given	The Promise
Isaiah 28:23; 51:4	Will You Not Listen?	The Word
Ezekiel 14:5	Recapture Me	The Word
Ezekiel 37:1-10	Valley of Dry Bones	The Word
Hosea 1–3	Song of Gomer	The Word
Amos 8:11	So Many Books	The Word
Zephaniah 3:20	I Will Bring You Home	The Word
Malachi 3:2	Who Can Abide?	The Word

The Gospels

The incarnation	To the Mystery	The Final Word
	The Final Word	The Final Word
The birth of Jesus	What Her Heart Remembered	The Promise
	Celebrate the Child	The Final Word
	Joseph's Song	The Promise/The Final Word
	Jacob's Star	The Promise
	Shepherd's Watch	The Promise

Scripture Reference	Song Title	Album
	We Will Find Him	The Promise
	Vicit Agnus Noster	The Promise
	Immanuel	The Promise
	Spirit of the Age	The Final Word
Blessing in the temple	Now That I've Held Him	The Early Works
Jesus in the temple	Voice of the Child	The Early Works
Baptism of Jesus	Meditation/Baptism	Scandalon
Calling the disciples	Things We Leave Behind	Poiema
Wedding at Cana	The Wedding	Scandalon
Jesus calms the sea	Asleep in the Bow	Come to the Cradle
Raising of the dead child	*Talitha Koumi*	Close Your Eyes
Ministry	The Nazarene	Scandalon
	The Gentle Healer	Scandalon
Triumphal entry	Ride On to Die	Known by the Scars
Last supper	Come to the Table	Known by the Scars
Jesus in the garden	In the Garden	Known by the Scars
Betrayal by Judas	Traitor's Look	Known by the Scars
Jesus dies on the cross	Why	Known by the Scars
	Cross of Glory	Known by the Scars
	Crown Him	Known by the Scars
Resurrection	Love Crucified Arose	The Early Works
Jesus comes to disciples	Stranger on the Shore	The Early Works

Specific Scriptures:

Matthew 19:14	Let the Children Come	Close Your Eyes
Matthew 19:16ff; Mark 2	What Will It Take to Keep You from Jesus?	Scandalon
Mark 3:21,22	God's Own Fool	Scandalon
John 2:12ff	The Lamb Is a Lion	Scandalon
John 8	Forgiving Eyes	Scandalon
John 13:4	The Basin and Towel	Poiema

Acts, Epistles, and the Book of Revelation

Paul, Timothy, and Barnabas	Bearers of the Light	Poiema
Romans 12:5	Flesh of His Flesh	Present Reality
1 Corinthians 1:19-25	Could It Be	Present Reality
1 Corinthians 11:23ff	Meditation #2, The Eucharist	Present Reality
2 Corinthians 8:9	Distressing Disguise	Present Reality
Galatians 3 (Romans 3:22)	That's What Faith Must Be	Present Reality
Ephesians 1:9	Live This Mystery	Present Reality
Ephesians 2:10	The Poem of Your Life	Poiema
Philippians 2:6-11	*Carmen Cristi*	The Final Word
Philippians 3:10	Know You in the Now	Present Reality
Colossians 3:15	In Stillness and Simplicity	Present Reality
Colossians 3:16	The Word	Present Reality
1 Thessalonians 4:13ff	Maranatha	Present Reality
Hebrews 5:7	He Was Heard	Known by the Scars
Revelation 1	The Unveiling	Unveiled Hope
Revelation 2; 3	To the Overcomers	Unveiled Hope
Revelation 4:8	Holy, Holy, Holy	Unveiled Hope
Revelation 4:11; 5:9-13	You Are Worthy	Unveiled Hope

Scripture Reference	Song Title	Album
Revelation 7:10-17	Salvation	Unveiled Hope
Revelation 12; 13	The Dragon	Unveiled Hope
	Dragonslayer	The Early Works
Revelation 15:3ff	The Song of the Lamb	Unveiled Hope
Revelation 18	The City of Doom	Unveiled Hope
Revelation 19	Hallelujah	Unveiled Hope
Revelation 21	The New Jerusalem	Unveiled Hope
Revelation 7:17; 21:4	He'll Wipe Away Your Tears	Sleep Sound in Jesus

The Albums:

Scandalon (Sparrow, 1985)

The Final Word (Sparrow, 1987)

Known By the Scars (Sparrow, 1989)

The Life (Sparrow, 1989)

Present Reality (Sparrow, 1988)

Sleep Sound in Jesus (Sparrow, 1989)

The Beginning (Sparrow, 1989)

The Way of Wisdom (Sparrow, 1990)

The Early Works (Benson Music, 1991)

The Promise (Sparrow, 1991)

The Word: Recapturing the Imagination (Sparrow, 1992)

The Ancient Faith (Sparrow, 1993)

Come to the Cradle (Sparrow, 1993)

Poiema (Sparrow, 1994)

Joy in the Journey: Ten Years of the Greatest Hits (Sparrow, 1994)

Brother to Brother (w/John Michael Talbot) (Myrrh, 1996)

Close Your Eyes So You Can See (Myrrh, 1996)

Unveiled Hope (Myrrh, 1997)

Katie, Maggie, Will, Nathan

Sunrise of Your Smile

*R*eject the worldly lie that says
That life lies always up ahead
Let power go before control becomes
a crust around your soul
Escape the hunger to possess
And soul-diminishing success
This world is full of narrow lives
I pray by grace your smile survives

For I would wander weary miles
Would welcome ridicule, my child
To simply see the sunrise of your smile
To see the light behind your eyes
The happy thought that makes you fly
Yes, I would wander weary miles
To simply see the sunrise of your smile

Now close your eyes so you can see
Your own unfinished memories
Now open them, for time is brief
And you'll be blest beyond belief
Now glance above you at the sky
There's beauty there to blind the eye
I ask all this then wait awhile
To see the dawning of your smile

Lyric from "Sunrise of Your Smile"/*Poiema*
Words by Michael Card/Music by Phil Naish
Used by permission

Epilogue

I hope this book has been a source of encouragement to you and your family. I urge you to read from the resource list provided, become aware of the present situation of education in our nation, and decide to make a difference in how you educate your children.

Now that the writing is over, I am returning to my first love and call—my family. I will be working diligently, just as many of you will be, to provide the best education for my children. Because of the time and energy required to be a wife and mother, I will not be able to respond to letters or accept speaking engagements. Like many of you, I am still learning a great deal and do not consider myself an "expert." But I do invite you to take advantage of the rich resources found in books and in your community. Above all else: Be encouraged!

—Susan Card

Other Good
Harvest House Reading

CLOSE YOUR EYES SO YOU CAN SEE
by Michael Card

Singer and songwriter Michael Card invites young ones to experience life as a child during the first century in the presence of Jesus. Ten stories with captivating, full-color illustrations by Stephen Marchesi bring the sights and sounds of Bible times to life.

SLEEP SOUND IN JESUS
by Michael Card

Designed to accompany Card's recording of lullabies by the same title, this 32-page, full-color children's picture book includes 16 lullabies, delightful illustrations, and special devotions for parents.

CHILDREN OF A GREATER GOD
by Terry Glaspey

Awaken your children's moral imaginations and lead them toward a life-long love for God. Keys to help prevent your children from being lured away from Christian values as they grow older.

GREAT BOOKS OF THE CHRISTIAN TRADITION
by Terry Glaspey

This collection provides brief introductions to more than 500 books. A perfect guide for individuals and families who want a richer understanding of their world and heritage through great literature.

TRAIN UP A CHILD
by Jean Lubin

They're short, they're easy to do. And they'll stick with your kids. Everything you need to have memorable, exciting family devotions—in one book!

STAY AT HOME MOM
by Donna Otto

This expanded and revised guide offers up-to-date information for mothers at home and those who want to be. Otto, with boundless enthusiasm for home and personal organization, takes on the challenges and highlights the rewards of being a stay-at-home mom.

WHAT YOUR CHILD NEEDS TO KNOW ABOUT GOD
by Ron Rhodes

In this practical resource, Ron Rhodes guides parents to communicate Bible doctrines children need to know. Clear "Pass It On" principles and nearly 100 illustrative stories allow parents to quickly access the information they need to teach Christian virtues.